CALL TO ARMS

By the same author:
GALLIPOLI AS I SAW IT

Call to Arms

From Gallipoli to the Western Front

JOSEPH MURRAY

WILLIAM KIMBER · LONDON

First published in 1980 by
WILLIAM KIMBER & CO. LIMITED
Godolphin House, 22a Queen Anne's Gate,
London, SW1H 9AE

ISBN 0 7183 0097 4

Photoset by
Specialised Offset Services Limited, Liverpool
and printed and bound in Great Britain by
Redwood Burn Limited, Trowbridge and Esher

Contents

List of illustrations

Dedicated to my old
comrade-in-arms
Captain D.N. Meneaud Lissenburg

Author's Note

During the Gallipoli Campaign I kept a rough diary on scraps of paper, some of which I sent home and others I kept with me. I kept a similar diary of my Western Front experiences. I had the remarkable experience of going through all the fighting at Gallipoli from the landing to the evacuation without a serious wound. On the Western Front I was not so lucky, for I was severely wounded at Gavrelle in 1917 and invalided home. Later in Spitzbergen, when I was engaged in mining exploration, I pieced the scraps of my diaries together and made a rough narrative, and later still I wrote this book from that material. The general historical background to the conflict at the point I was plunged into it may be summarised as follows:

At the beginning of the 1914 war, Turkey's position was that of an unstable neutral. The Young Turks were in power, a revolutionary party not entirely acceptable to the British Government. The German Military Mission under Liman von Sanders dominated the Turkish Army; the British Military Mission had rather less control of the Turkish Navy. Then, towards the end of September 1914, a German officer authorised the closing of the Dardanelles by mines, a flagrant breach of Turkish neutrality, and a month later Turkey was at war on the German side. The importance to Britain was this: the Black Sea was now effectively sealed off from the Mediterranean and the vital supply line to her Russian ally was cut.

By April 1915 the war in France and Flanders had reached a trench-bound stalemate. The vast Russian armies had suffered defeat at Tannenberg and the Masurian Lakes; they wanted help in the form of arms and ammunition; and they wanted the Turks distracted from their campaigns in the Caucasus. If Russia collapsed, Germany's most serious worry, that of fighting a war on two fronts, was gone. The situation revived an old idea of Winston Churchill, the First Lord of the Admiralty, an operation to force the Dardanelles and seize Constantinople. Kitchener made it clear that he could spare no troops from the main battlefields, and so the first plans were for a primarily naval assault.

In March 1915 a combined Franco-British force attempted to sail up the Dardanelles; as they reached the Narrows and victory seemed in sight, three battleships fell victims to mines, and the operation was temporarily halted and finally given up. It was now clear that the Navy could not do the whole job themselves. A combined operation was planned and launched on 25th April, 1915. The command of the Army was given to General Ian Hamilton, who was told by Kitchener: 'If the Fleet gets through, Constantinople will fall of itself and you will have won not a battle, but the war'.

In the weeks following the naval attack, the Turks had not been idle. The command of the force defending the Dardanelles was given to Liman von Sanders; he had six divisions, and he disposed them with extraordinary skill. The Allied Force consisted of 75,000 men: the Anzac Corps – two divisions, one Australian and one New Zealand; 29th British Division; a French division; and the Royal Naval Division, to which Joseph Murray belonged. The Anzacs landed at Gaba Tepe; 29th Division at Cape Helles, to be joined by the French, who had made an unsuccessful attempt to establish a bridgehead at Kum Kale, and the Royal Naval Division, which had first staged a diversionary mock-landing further up the peninsula, to keep the Turkish troops widely dispersed. The Cape Helles landing was reasonably successful, but Mount Achi Baba, which dominated the whole bridgehead, was not captured in the first few days as planned, and indeed never was. The Anzacs only established themselves on a narrow strip of cliffside which was overlooked at close quarters by the Turkish positions. Attempts to break out of the two separated bridgeheads were unsuccessful and incurred heavy loss of life.

The situation was again a stalemate, but the casualties continued to mount. It was decided that the only way out of the deadlock was a fresh landing, to be made at Suvla Bay, further to the north. General Hamilton now had 120,000 men available in all; the Turks numbered about the same. On 6th August a force of 20,000 men was landed at Suvla Bay; in spite of their taking the Turks partially by surprise, and tremendous support from the Anzacs, at the end of twenty-four hours they had barely advanced two miles. It was not enough. The battle dragged on for a further three weeks but achieved practically nothing.

In October, the first plans for evacuation were discussed; by December, rumours had spread round the fighting men. The Anzac and Suvla Bay positions were abandoned on the 19th December. The four divisions at Cape Helles held on alone against twenty-one Turkish divisions. On 8th January 1916 the last British troops were safely evacuated from Cape Helles. The Gallipoli campaign was over.

CHAPTER ONE

Called to Arms

I was born on 8th October 1896, the son of a Scots miner who lived and worked in north-west Durham. Educated at Leases School, Burnopfield, I reached the highest class by the time I was eleven years old and entered and succeeded in passing what in those days was called the Labour Examination. This entitled me on reaching the age of twelve to leave school provided it was proved to the education authorities that it was essential to provide additional money for the home. In north-west Durham the schools had an annual holiday in the first week of October known as Blackberry week, and my schooling days ended at the beginning of the holiday But instead of gathering blackberries, I began work at South Garesfield Colliery a few days before my twelfth birthday at the union rate for the job, one penny an hour for a shift of ten hours per day. I remember this princely wage, as the custom of the mining families was that a boy was allowed to keep his first week's pay – in my case, one day at tenpence, less twopence stoppages. From then onwards each member of the family handed over all his earnings, however much they were, to Mother who was the official exchequer and saw to all the requirements of the household, which, even in those days was quite a tricky job.

Suitably dressed for the job, hob-nailed boots and old clothes, (I was quite grown up before I owned any new clothes; being the youngest boy of the family, I had to make do with the cast-offs of my older brothers) I reported for work as instructed, at the Drift mouth, at 6 a.m. after walking over a mile through the snow. I was instructed to collect a bucket of very thick grease and to apply a little to every sheave in the middle of the track and also those on the side that accommodated the 'Tail' rope between the drift-mouth and the terminus a mile or so underground, but as soon as the main rope moved, I was to go at once to one of the frequent recesses and to stay there until the train of tubs passed. If the train was at the in-bye terminus there was plenty of time to do this, as the refuge-holes as they were called were never too far apart. However one never knew for certain where the train actually was. It may have been stopped on its way in or out for some reason or other, so the instruction had to be adhered to at all times for safety sake.

Of course, I was aware of all this as I had spent many hours underground before actually starting work. At this particular colliery, there were five seams of coal ranging from two feet eight inches to only sixteen inches thick, at different levels in the hillside. The upper ones were approached directly and the lower ones by a deep shaft. In each case when the hewer had extracted the coal (a mere pencil mark compared to some of the seams in the country, but of a very good quality), there were two or three feet of rock to be blasted to make a gallery roughly four feet high to allow the tub to be filled, provided the front pair of wheels were allowed to overrun the end of the track.

When my father was supervising the blasting at the coal-face that took place after every shift, I, on my return from school at 4.30 p.m., would rush down the hill with a small white cotton bag which contained several slices of bread and butter known to the miner as his 'bait'. I also carried a tin can of boiling hot tea with a couple of hard-boiled eggs therein. A woollen stocking leg around the can kept the contents fairly warm. By the time I reached the coal-face my father would have all the rock ready for blasting with different lengths of fuse. It was my pride and joy to ignite them one by one and then hurry to a place of safety some little distance away to await the bangs. The resultant fumes – we call it reek – prevented further work until they had cleared. During this interval, dinner was served. I was always given one of the eggs and thoroughly enjoyed the whole evening. As a special treat my father allowed me occasionally to dig at the coal-face, sometimes I helped to drill the holes in the canch, as we called the rock. I was training to become a miner and my instructor was recognised to be an expert by the mining community.

I had grown-up long before I left school but now I was actually a wage earner and considered myself worthy of my keep. Very soon I had a very frisky galloway pony called Vulcan that seemed to enjoy my childish prank of getting under his belly and I would sometimes ease him off the ground, to the delight of the other pony drivers. We would collect our galloways from the stables and ride bare-back to our respective drifts, quite an easy task as all the ponies insisted on a slow walk up the hill. After completion of the day's work, though, the moment they saw daylight there was no holding them; it was full gallop down the hill and many times the galloways reached the stables and were hosed down and curry-combed long before their drivers arrived.

In my village, Lintz, as in most of the mining villages in the area, there was only one road and this wound its way between the rows of drab miners' hovels from the mineshaft to the cemetery. It was Hobson's choice; sons followed their fathers down the mine and often died with them when there was an accident; sometimes whole families were lost in an explosion.

As time went on, one was upgraded, not by seniority but by strength and ability. Payment was by results and the harder you worked and the more risks you took, the more you earned. Boys became men at an early age and men were old and feeble long before they reached what in normal life should have been their prime. Miners are a tough breed; they have to be. They know the risks and accept them as a matter of course.

One fine day early in June 1914 my brother Tom who had served his five years in the Royal Navy, left for his month of Special Reserve training. He jokingly referred to it as his annual holiday. I was working with him at the time in the Victoria seam and, as his training time approached, our conversation always veered round to his belief that Germany had been for a long time preparing for war with England. With the launching of the 'Dreadnought' class warships and the subsequent deepening of the Kiel canal, German intentions were now quite clear. Moreover, during Tom's service he had taken part in the Naval manoeuvres in the North Sea in 1912 with a mock invasion by the German High Seas Fleet. In his diary he had written:

> A foreign fleet escorting transports could land troops on the east coast of England between Sunderland and Cromer, notwithstanding the fact that a fleet comprising half as many battleships and cruisers over and above those of the invading fleet was patrolling the whole of the coast.

There was no doubt in Tom's mind that war with Germany was imminent. He advised me to join the Territorials so that if the Germans invaded and I was captured carrying arms, I would be treated as a prisoner-of-war and not shot as a spy.

As time went on we heard that Tom had rejoined his old ship. HMS *Good Hope*. He and all at home were delighted. He had served on her when Sir Percy Scott had made her his flagship on that memorable sixty-thousand miles cruise. Our pleasure was, however, cut short. The summer Naval manoeuvres had almost ended and Tom was due to come home but the sky had darkened and war clouds had blotted out the July sunshine.

On Thursday, 28th July the Austrian-Hungarian heir presumptive, the Archduke Franz Ferdinand had been directing army manoeuvres and was on his way to an official welcome by the Mayor of Sarajevo, the capital of Bosnia. The route to the town hall entailed the cortege of four cars crossing three bridges over the river Milgiazka. As the cars were about to cross the first bridge, a bomb was thrown. The Archduke and his wife, the Duchess of Hohenberg, escaped injury, but an attendant in the following car was wounded. The suite arrived at the town hall without further incident and after the speech of welcome the Archducal pair decided to visit the wounded attendant in the hospital. As a measure of safety, the route was changed but unfortunately, just before eleven o'clock, the driver of the leading car, keeping to the original route, turned into Franz Joseph street instead of proceeding straight on. The mistake caused a momentary stoppage during which a nineteen-year-old student, Gavrilo Princip, rushed forward and fired two revolver shots at point blank range. The first killed the Archduke and the second mortally wounded the Duchess who had tried to shield her husband.

Those two shots, on the Archducal pair's fourteenth anniversary of their wedding, set the world on fire. The Austrian government were convinced that the assassination was inspired by the Serbian government and promptly sent a brusque ultimatum, knowing full well that the terms were impossible. Serbia had long been a thorn in Austria's side and now Austria demanded her pound of flesh. Russia, who had an understanding with France, made it quite clear that she would not stand aside while a small Slav state was threatened with extinction. Germany, an ally of Austria, had requested permission from King Albert to go through Belgium to attack France but this was refused. England had pledged France that she would not allow the German Fleet to enter the Channel to attack French territory; that was the limit of England's involvement until Germany invaded Belgium, who relied on our hundred years friendship to come to her aid.

Prime Minister H.H. Asquith, in his speech in the House of Commons on 6th August said:

'If I am asked what we are fighting for I can reply in two sentences. In the first place to fulfil a solemn international obligation – an obligation which, if it had been entered into between private persons in the ordinary concerns of life, would have been regarded as an obligation, not only in law but of honour, which no self-respecting man could possibly have repudiated. I say, secondly, we are fighting to vindicate the principle, in these days when material force sometimes seems to be the dominant influence in the development of mankind, that small nationalities are not to be crushed, in defiance of international good faith, by the arbitrary will of a strong and overmastering power.'

The consensus was that a war on such a scale could not possibly last long and it would be over by Christmas, though Lord Kitchener thought otherwise. Soon posters were seen at Post Offices, in newspapers and on hoardings asking for men to volunteer for service in the Army for a period of three years or more if needed. The following appeared in the *Daily Telegraph* on 11th August 1914:

YOUR KING AND COUNTRY
NEED YOU!
– A CALL TO ARMS!
An addition of 100,000 men to His Majesty's Regular Army is immediately necessary in the present grave National Emergency. Lord Kitchener is confident that this appeal will be at once responded to by all those who have the safety of our Empire at heart;
TERMS OF SERVICE
General Service for a period of 3 years or until the War is concluded.
Age of enlistment between 19 and 30.
HOW TO JOIN
Full information can be obtained at any Post Office in the United Kingdom or at any Military Depot.
GOD SAVE THE KING.

Up to the end of August the war seemed to be a long way away, apart from the flagwaving, but then it became known that the British Expeditionary Force had been forced to retire from the Belgian town of Mons to escape encirclement; it was an orderly retirement but the casualty list told of the severity of the fighting. More posters calling for volunteers for Kitchener's Army; the age of enlistment was now eighteen. Queues formed at the recruitment offices and patriotism ran wild. Selection was eclectic and hundreds were turned away. On Tuesday, 6th October, after a hard day's work, I walked the eight miles to Elswick and volunteered to join the Royal Naval Volunteer Reserve on board HMS *Calliope* on the Tyne. Winston Churchill had called for young men to operate in Naval brigades. I remember Tom telling me of the wonderful contribution of a Naval brigade during the South African war, how they mounted some smaller Naval guns on carriages and took them ashore and joined in the fighting with the land force.

Bearing this in mind and the general belief that the war might not last long, I felt that if I joined the Army I would have many months of training before seeing any action, whereas in the Navy I

(*left*) Myself at Blandford Camp in February 1915, just before leaving for active service, and (*right*) my brother Tom.

would maybe see some action at once. After the interview I was told to report on board on Saturday the 10th for medical examination; this I did and passed it. I was very disappointed when I was told to go home and await further instructions but fortunately I did not have to wait long. I received instructions to report on board on Monday the 19th for draft to the Crystal Palace.

At the Palace we were first allocated in the Monkey House, and subsequently issued with, sailors' uniform minus 'dicky' but that did not prevent the mad rush to the photographer's studio in Penge. The food at the Palace was luscious and plentiful, supplied by Joe Lyons. To us new recruits, the Palace was the 'Glass House', to the Navy it was HMS Victory VI. Within the grounds we were square-bashing all day long but outside we were idolized by the people of London. On 31st October there was a call for volunteers to join the *Hood*, whatever that meant. I readily put up my hand and was warned to stand by for draft to HMS *Vivid*, actually Devonport Naval Barracks. This meant I could not go 'ashore' but had to remain within shouting distance. This did not worry me unduly as I thought I would soon be on the move, which I fervently desired. By the following night I was with the *Hood* Battalion, Royal Naval Division. (Victory IV).

During the days that followed, the conversation among the 'Pukka' sailors was mainly about the *Good Hope* and *Monmouth*. There was a very strong rumour that both these vessels had been sunk in the Southern Pacific, off Coronel. Admiral Sir Christopher Cradock was engaged in playing tag with a squadron of the Imperial German Navy under Admiral von Spee, far superior in speed and gun-power. To redress the balance the Admiralty had dispatched the old, obsolete battleship *Canopus*, a slow vessel of only seventeen knots but considerably superior to the Germans in fire-power and range. Cradock realised that at seventeen knots he had no hope of catching the German squadron. He therefore pushed on after the Germans without waiting for the *Canopus*. When he did intercept the enemy, he did not shadow them until the *Canopus*, less than twenty hours' sailing away, could head them off, but engaged them immediately, notwithstanding his serious inferiority in gun-power and range. *Good Hope* and *Monmouth*, out-ranged and out-

Lieutenant-Commander Freyberg with officers of the 'Hood' Battalion at Blandford Camp in February 1915. *From left to right: back row:* Lt Arthur Asquith, Lt Jacobs, Lt Waller, Lt Shadbolt; *middle row:* Lt Nelson, Lt Rupert Brooke, Lt Egerton, Lt Dodge, Lt Denis Browne, Lt the Hon Charles Lister, Lt Martin, Lt Gamage, Lt Cassey, Lt QM Nobbs; *front row:* Gilliard, Lt Ferguson, Lt-Commanders Freyberg, Parsons and Graham, Lt-Col Quilter, Lt-Cdr Burnett, Lt-Cdr Daglish, Lt Hughes, Lt the Hon N. Hood, Lt-Cdr Hedderwick.

gunned, were sunk within an hour and one hundred years of invincibility since the battle of Trafalgar had gone to the bottom of the sea with them – and my brother, too. To me, everything that Tom did was manly, and honest, I worshipped him though he did not know it. There would come a time when I would avenge him.

5th December 1914

The battalion moved to a partially erected camp in the wilderness some three miles from that quaint old town of Blandford in Dorset. Some of the huts had roofs and some had not but, in a few days we had enough of them ship-shape for our requirements. We were out on the downs all day training. If it rained – and it did – we got plastered with mud and chalk and were expected to get dried out the best way we could. No one thought of building drying rooms. We had one small oil heater in each hut which gave off less heat than a miner's safety lamp and we almost froze to death. Within a few days the space between the huts became a quagmire. Still, it was an open-air life and the healthy, envigorating Dorset air was just what we needed to make us fighting fit; only the fit survived! After the turn of the New Year, we changed our navy blue uniforms for khaki military ones, with the exception of the peakless naval cap which we retained, naval type in shape but khaki in colour.

Saturday, 27th February

Dies datus. A truly appointed day, ever to be remembered. We paraded in the pouring rain at six in the evening wearing our recently acquired sun helmets. Sou'westers would have been more appropriate. Lieutenant-Colonel Arnold Quilter gave the order we had waited so long to hear: 'The battalion will move off in column of route, A Company leading.' Without the slightest fuss the battalion moved off, destination Dardanelles. We had expected to entrain at Blandford station but after two hours' marching in the pouring rain over the downs, we boarded the awaiting train at Shillingstone, soaked to the skin but extremely happy.

Sunday, 28th February

At three in the morning we arrived alongside the *Grantully Castle*, a vessel of 7,592 tons, lying at Avonmouth. When we had eventually loaded our equipment we received orders to stay aboard. To make sure we did so, sentries were posted at the head of the gangway. Less than twenty hours after leaving camp at Blandford, the mooring lines were cast off and we sailed slowly away from England leaving less than a dozen on the quayside to wave us '*Bon Voyage*'.

What had Fate in store for us? If we could have looked forward, say, four years or so, how many of us would have fallen from the path we were now taking? How many were to return? Maybe it is merciful not to see too far ahead.

Sailing down the Bristol Channel as the sun was setting was a thrilling experience. I had noticed the sunsets of late; they had been sombre with troubled skies but this night's sunset would be for ever remembered because for me it was first of a new era. I was leaving with a nasty task to do and my heart was heavy. Travellers and poets in truth and fiction describe their feelings on leaving their homeland but it is sufficient to say that neither traveller nor poet can adequately describe the parting. The sky had been beautiful all day but now a tremendously long light-pink and orange cloud lay across its soft blue vault and pale mauve clouds floated above the horizon, only suddenly to change to red and orange, surmounted by soft saffron, as the sun went down. As I watched, I longed to be an artist capable of portraying adequately the scene so vivid and so real. Awed by the beauty of such surroundings I thought that if the gates of Paradise could be more beautiful or stupendous than this earthly sunset, I hoped that at some future date I might make acquaintance with them. It is usually agreed however, that the life of a soldier practically annuls all such heavenly anticipations.

A bugle call brought me back to earth with a bump. We appeared to be clear of the Bristol Channel and our escort of five destroyers were continually signalling and coming in close. How gracefully these vessels cut the sea and how neat they looked compared with the five transports in the convoy. The lights of England were sinking out of view – for how long I wondered? I stayed on deck until a stiff breeze forced me to go down below, with the idea of turning in, but the stench nauseated me. I found my own hammock and carried it back on deck. Someone had borrowed my blankets so, with the hammock as my only covering, I slept on deck until rudely awakened by the crew who thought it funny to turn upon my school-boy friend and me the three-inch hoses they were using to wash down the deck.

I had slept reasonably well but did not feel so good when I began to walk about. The sea was choppy and the old tub could not make up her mind whether to go over the huge waves or underneath them. Sometimes she appeared to be going sideways, with the result that most of us youngsters spent the early hours looking over the port side one moment and the starboard rail the next. I suppose the Skipper had made the usual entry in the log book: 'Ship holding on course'. I was more concerned in holding on to my breakfast, but the sea, that choppy, hungry, cruel sea, claimed it in the end. The old tub was trying her utmost to pitch the lot of us into the ditch. The pitching and rolling and all the other antics continued all day and night and most of the next day. It was not until late evening of the third day that she got back on an even keel. How relieved I was when the lights on the Spanish coast came into view, the crew said they were on Cap Finisterre. As we steamed close in to the coast of Portugal the sea became much calmer and the weather decidedly warmer.

In spite of the frugal victuals, I felt fine. It must have been the sea air and the biscuits and cheese, plus an occasional mug of cocoa bought from the crew late at night. This additional mug of concentrated vitamins was not allowed, and to be caught buying it meant extra fatigues.

Monday, 8th March

At three o'clock in the afternoon we anchored in the Grand Harbour, Malta, followed in by two French warships. Our silver band struck up the 'Marseillaise' followed by 'God save the King'. Our entire ship's company and the crews of both French warships stood to attention until the band finished playing and then everyone cheered loudly and waved their caps. It was a rousing welcome; at last someone was pleased to see us. At eleven o'clock the following morning we steamed out of the Grand Harbour and did not see land again until we reached the Cyclades, those numerous islands that lie between the Mediterranean and the Aegean, the following afternoon. The weather was glorious.

Thursday, 11th March

It was late in the afternoon when we steamed into Mudros harbour, Lemnos; we were now less than fifty miles from the Dardanelles. Sheltering in this huge deep-sea anchorage were many British and French warships ranging from the most powerful of them all, the *Queen Elizabeth* with her 15-inch guns, to the numerous small craft that appeared to be always on the move. We anchored quite close to the Russian cruiser, *Askold*, promptly nick-named 'Woodbine Willie' because of her five slender funnels. Close by lay the French warship *Henri IV* – this ship, by the look of her was built during Henri IV's reign, for she had the appearance and style of a castle afloat. Her freeboard astern appeared almost awash, her turrets high above the water and her towers higher still.

The following day we landed. It was nice to be on dry land again; one felt more free and able to move about. Somehow the air was different and the sun was very hot; there was no shade anywhere. Time had stood still here and it amused me to observe an elderly Greek manipulating a wooden plough drawn by two oxen. He was making a really good furrow but the pace was painfully slow, but he was happy. Each day the routine was much to the pattern of the first day. We went over the side by way of rope ladders and into the ship's boats, rowed ourselves ashore, scrambled out and lined the beach to attack the mythical enemy. After we had cleared the beach we got into some sort of formation and marched inland, closely followed by supposedly friendly Greeks offering for sale chocolate, oranges and figs, obviously brought from the Turkish mainland. We were supposed to be a secret army and yet, here we were, fooling about on a Greek island only some forty-seven miles from the Gallipoli Peninsula whilst at least some of the island's inhabitants were obviously in constant contact with Greece and Asia Minor.

Thursday, 18th March

We were recalled from the island and within an hour – at six in the evening – were steaming out of the harbour. A cool breeze was blowing as we steered an easterly course for a little while and then veered to the north. We were on our way to the Dardanelles. Action at last. We were all very excited; although no orders had been given, we knew that Russia was desperately short of war matériel but had ample grain, whilst the Western Allies had arms to spare but were short of foodstuffs. Our task would be to force the Dardanelles so that an exchange could be made. Furthermore, the Grand Duke Nicholas, the Commander-in-Chief of the Russian armies, had asked the Allies to make some demonstration against Turkey so as to relieve the pressure of the Turkish armies on the Russians in the Caucasus.

Friday, 19th March

We arrived in the Gulf of Xeros in the region of Microsaros and Saros Islands at the head of the Gulf and, as we steamed slowly down the western coast of the Gallipoli Peninsula, we were ordered to man the rails in full battle order, which we did, our bayonets glistening in the sun. We were close inshore and about to land. Some of my platoon were pointing to the cliffs where they said they could see Turks moving about but, although I peered very hard, I could not observe anyone for certain.

HMS *Dublin* seemed to be escorting us towards the entrance to the Straits. The *Queen Elizabeth*, lying well out to sea, was bombarding the shore and destroyers were cruising round and round. Many ships were firing and great clouds of smoke stretched across the whole area. As we arrived at the entrance to the most famous straits in the world, many more warships came into view, each firing at its own target, numerous destroyers and torpedo-craft continuing to circle round and round.

In full view of the Turks, we expected the order to disembark at any moment but the order was not given this day. For more than a couple of hours we remained on view, watching, waiting and wondering. No doubt the Turks were wondering exactly where and when we would strike; as invaders it was for us to choose the time and place. There was not much choice of landing place but, even so, the decision was ours. The Turks had to remain where they were, ready to defend their homeland.

Our warships had been shelling the coastal forts and demolition parties had landed at this very spot, at Sedd-el-Bahr and Kum Kale two weeks ago. Thus the Turks had received ample warning and no doubt were ready, nicely hidden in and on top of those high cliffs. We had come over two thousand miles, opened the gate and strolled up the garden path. The door stood wide open but instead of entering, we turned about and left. Twenty hours after leaving Mudros harbour we were back at anchor there. The naval attack to force the Straits had failed. We had lost three ships – *Ocean, Bouvet* and *Irresistible* – and the *Inflexible* was badly holed, not by gunfire, but all by mines. The channel had been swept again and again; whether the sweepers had missed these mines or whether they were free and coming down with the current, we did not know, but it was clear that so long as the Turks held the banks of the Straits, mines would always be a menace. Before the Navy had any hopes of passing through the Straits, the Gallipoli Peninsula must be occupied. The Navy could not force the Straits alone.

Wednesday, 24th March

After two weeks' stay at Lemnos, at six o'clock in the evening we sailed for Egypt. Rumour was that the Navy had abandoned the idea of forcing the Straits alone; it would have to be a joint affair with the Army. Apparently all our transports were not loaded to suit this proposition and we were going to Egypt so that this error could be rectified. We arrived at Port Said at seven o'clock on the morning of the 27th and went ashore almost immediately as a general working party setting up tents on the sands to form a camp. The battalion disembarked the following morning and occupied the camp; there were twenty-seven men allocated to my tent; a dozen at the most could get inside an ordinary bell-tent so the remainder had to sleep outside. During the day it was extremely hot but after sundown it was quite cold. A soldier's day in the Middle East begins very early but all parades finish early and we were free to go visiting the Arab quarter in particular, if we so desired. The

Military Police had other ideas as usual. On the whole the training during our stay was in no way arduous and the food was quite nice and plentiful.

Saturday, 3rd April

We were inspected by the Commander-in-Chief, Sir Ian Hamilton, on the sands outside the town. Immediately after the march past we had to break step as the sands began to roll; like the waves of the sea. It was like trying to walk on a spring mattress. The 'Anson' battalion left immediately for Alexandria. They were to act as a working party for the 29th Division who had apparently just arrived. Like us, their transports had to be reloaded to suit the job in hand, to land on open beaches.

Easter Sunday, 4th April

Out and about very early in the morning doing a little firing practice. We placed six-inch square tiles along the bank of the canal for use as targets. Whilst firing we could hear a *muezzin* calling the faithful from a minaret in the town. I'm afraid the *muezzin's* call to prayer this morning was not heeded as most of his people were watching us, panicstricken. I think they thought the Turkish Army was on the other side of the canal. The Arabs are normally extremely garrulous, and Bedlam, compared with a mob of excited Arabs, would be a Victorian vicarage tea-party. Long after we had finished firing they were still highly excited and looking very worried. Incidentally, the Turks, probably a small patrol, did approach the canal three days later but were beaten off. Our composite force at El Kantara was in no way troubled.

Saturday, 10th April

Early in the morning, with a cool breeze blowing, we steamed towards the open sea on our way to the Dardanelles again, knowing full well that our reception would not be as peaceful as on our last visit. The element of surprise – so essential for this sort of enterprise – had been lost long ago. Still, we were young and thirsting for adventure and were not unduly worried. In fact, we were looking forward to our new adventure. As we steamed slowly past de

Lesseps' monument at the entrance to the canal, I reflected that his works were of construction whereas ours would be of destruction – human and material. His name would live for ever; how soon would ours be forgotten? Once clear of the breakwater, the sea was rough and gradually got worse. The storm reached its peak on the thirteenth when we lost the lighter we were towing. We picked it up the following morning near the island of Kos and proceeded on our way to Lemnos.

Thursday, 15th April

A fancy dress ball was held in the afternoon. The most original costumes were to be seen. I was astonished to find myself gazing at a young 'lady' clad in the finest coloured silks, looking very seductive and being chased by an almost naked Zulu warrior whose feet were even larger than those of the 'lady'. Another chap was clad in armour made from biscuit tins, complete with shield and a sort of hatchet. 'Hood' battalion commander, Colonel A.G. Quilter, came forward and said: 'We will now give the prizes; tomorrow we will give the Turks hell. By tomorrow I mean that in a few days' time we are going to land on the Gallipoli Peninsula. The eyes of the world will be upon us and the whole course of the war will depend on the success of our effort. We have to succeed and take Constantinople from the Turks. If we find it is impossible to land on the toe, we will try the neck, the Bulair Lines or, failing there, at Enos.' Now we knew officially where we are going. We had known unofficially before we left England; the whole world must have known.

Friday, 16th April

As we entered Mudros harbour at seven o'clock in the morning four transports, one of them the *Royal George*, were leaving. We turned about in the harbour and followed in their wake. After a little while a destroyer came in very close. We turned about at once and headed back towards Lemnos. Rumour had it that a Turkish gunboat had intercepted one of our transports, the *Manitou* and had fired three torpedoes at such close range that, fortunately, all three had gone harmlessly under her keel. After some time, we – like Dick

Whittington – turned again and at dusk arrived in Trebuki Bay, Scyros. Here we were told that one of our destroyers had chased the Turkish gunboat and ran her ashore on the island of Chios.

CHAPTER TWO

Gallipoli

Friday, 23rd April

This was the original date for the landing on the Gallipoli Peninsula but on the 21st a strong wind sprang up and continued the whole day and the following night. Calm weather was essential for the landing of troops from open boats and each boat would have to make several journeys. In consequence, the landing was postponed for forty-eight hours.

Although we did not know it at the time, this was an extension of life for many of the troops assembled in the area – a further two days to make peace with our Maker, but for Sub-Lieutenant Rupert Brooke of 'A' Company, 'Hood' battalion, the sands had run out, as he knew they would. He died from sunstroke and severe blood poisoning from an insect bite on the lip, at a quarter to five in the evening on board the hospital ship *Duguay Trouin* lying in Trebuki bay, Scyros. That evening seven of his brother officers, with the aid of the men of his own platoon, dug his grave high up in an olive grove with Mount Khotrilas at its head and flanked by the mountains of Pephko and Komaro. His poem 'The Soldier' conveys his thoughts to the world in no uncertain manner:

If I should die, think only this of me;
That there's some corner of a foreign field
That is for ever England. There shall be
In that rich earth a richer dust concealed;
A dust whom England bore, shaped, made aware,
Gave, once, her flowers to love, her ways to roam,
A body of England's, breathing English air,
Washed by the rivers, blest by suns of home.

Saturday, 24th April

The transports in the harbour began to move. More than one hundred men from the 'Hood' battalion, with previous sea service, had already left to serve as landing and beach parties. It was late in the evening when we steamed out of Trebuki Bay to the sound of cheering from the ships we passed; they were soon to follow, into the jaws of death, a one-way journey.

Sunday, 25th April

Just before dawn we appeared to have arrived at our rendezvous in the vicinity of Xeros Island at the north-east end of the gulf of that name. The ship's engines had considerably slowed and there was no visible wake. At sunrise two of the warships began bombarding the Peninsula while the fleet of transports lay in the background waiting to go in and land their troops. The warships continued to bombard the Bulair Lines and this game of the cat watching the mouse continued all day. We knew there were troops on the shore; the Turks knew there were troops on the transports lying off-shore; waiting to land. The warships continued to lob their shells at the shore; we only stood and stared.

In the early afternoon, my section leader, Leading Seaman Harris, came to ask for thirty volunteers that were good swimmers. I was the first of his section he met – volunteer number one. The remaining twenty-nine were soon lined up and taken below at once to the clothing store and issued with brand new canvas slippers, new cardigan and woollen cap-comforters, then to the armoury for two bandoliers each holding fifty rounds. Afterwards came the briefing. We thirty men were going to be towed to within 800 yards of the shore. From there, we would row ourselves the rest of the way. We were the bait and were to attract the enemy's attention so that they would be left in no doubt that this was the spot chosen for a landing. The fleet of transports had been in view all day so we could be sure of a warm reception.

The Australian and New Zealanders had already gone ashore at Gaba Tepe, a little farther down the coast and the 29th Division had landed at Cape Helles at the toe of the Peninsula. Our own little demonstration would force the Turkish Command to hold the main body of their troops, known to be in the Bulair area, in readiness to contest a threatened landing. In the meantime, our troops already ashore would make good their footholds, and could be reinforced.

At nine in the evening the 'suicide' party – as we were called – were given as much steaming hot cocoa as we could drink. Normally we did not get anything to eat or drink after tea. A wit referred to it as 'The Last Supper'. A little before 10 p.m. we were ordered to man the ship's boat riding in the swell alongside. We had been warned that there would be no talking and absolute silence must be maintained at all costs. I nipped down Jacob's ladder fairly quickly as I felt that if the chap following me stood on my fingers, I might forget the ban on talking and maybe say something rude.

When we were all aboard we eased off, the muffled oars slipped into the water and the suicide party was on its way to Constantinople. The oars cut the water as if they were handled by ghosts – not a sound, not a light anywhere. Away from the shelter of our transport we felt very cold as we had left our tunics on board. Chief Petty Officer Milton had followed me down and he instructed me to go to the bow and keep a sharp look-out while he took up his position astern. I kept my eyes fixed straight ahead; it seemed a long way before we were cast off. More than half-an-hour, at a guess, after we had left the transport, a brilliant flash followed by a deafening noise broke the silence and revealed our position. A salvo from a warship maybe a mile or so away, but the flash lit up the whole coast line, now looking very close. I slung my rifle into a firing position, felt for my bandoliers and prepared to jump. I had seen the cliffs a moment or so before but it was now darker than ever.

Our boat struck something and swung away to starboard. It was so dark that there were times when I could not even see the sea. Were we lost? If it was our intention to land, why didn't we? If we were to attract attention only, why not a few rounds of rapid fire? We had rifles and a hundred rounds of ammunition each. If they were not to be used, why on earth did we bring them with us?

It was early in the morning when we came back on board the

Grantully Castle. How we found the old tub I shall never know as ship's cutters do not carry any navigational instruments. We couldn't see the sea, let alone the stars. We had been out in an open boat for many hours and were so cold that it was most difficult to climb Jacob's ladder. At once we were given beautiful piping-hot cocoa – as much as we could drink. During this time, Lieutenant B.C. Freyberg of 'A' Company had swum from the other ship's boat and ignited flares on the beach in two different places. He swam most of the way back before being picked up by the cutter manned by Lieutenant E.W. Nelson, who was searching for him. Only a super-man could have survived so long in that icy-cold sea. He was awarded the DSO and he certainly earned it.

Tuesday, 27th April

It would appear that our demonstration has ended. We have steamed down the coast to Gaba Tepe. The Australian and New Zealanders did not appear to have advanced very far inland and we could see fighting taking place on the slopes running down to the beach on both flanks. There were many shells bursting on the hills beyond and more on the beach and in the sea. It was difficult to assess the position exactly from a distance but we could see troops fighting on the beach on both flanks of the cove as we steamed close in down the coast. On arrival at Cape Helles at first glance the position seemed to be much the same as at Gaba Tepe, but as we moved round the cape things looked better. Fighting was taking place all over the toe of the Peninsula and the Fleet were banging away as usual. At about 4.30 p.m. our troops on shore advanced apparently unopposed by the sound of things, more than a couple of miles down the sloping plain towards the foothills of Achi Baba where the Turks had prepared a defensive position it would seem.

Wednesday, 28th April

Steaming up the coast again we took up a position off Gaba Tepe. The situation on shore looked much the same as it did yesterday; rifle fire and almost continuous shelling. During the night though, and on the following morning, the Australians and the New Zealanders made some progress up the very steep hills and the rifle fire and shelling greatly increased. The warships were sending over salvo after salvo as we watched the shells bursting on the various ridges. Later on in the afternoon we sailed away down the coast again to Cape Helles and landed on the Peninsula, taking up a position on the slope above 'W' beach.

At daybreak the enemy shelling was so accurate that we were forced over the ridge and to dig funk holes in the long grass behind the firing line. There was a lot of sniping and several of our chaps became casualties. The firing line at this stage was not a continuous line, just a series of outposts strung here and there marking our extended position across the toe of the Peninsula. As we were the only support troops available, we were at the beck and call of the forward line. At any sign of activity by the enemy on any part of the extended line, we were dispatched to meet the expected attack or to fill the numerous gaps caused by the pitiful shortage of troops at this part of the campaign. There were no reserves at all; the pride of the gallant 29th Division were lying dead on and around the beaches.

Saturday, 1st May

Throughout the whole day we moved about in the open in small groups trying to turf out the snipers who were pestering us. We did not have much success. We probed the scrub and surrounded the small clumps of trees but still the snipers found their targets. The stray bullets added to our difficulties in defining the direction of the sniping.

Shortly after ten o'clock in the evening the Turks attacked. We moved quickly across to the right and took up a position across the Achi Baba *nullah*; 'Anson' battalion went to the extreme right to assist the French, who were hard-pressed. For quite a little while it was touch and go – we broke up the attack again and again but still they came on and were mown down at almost point-blank range. It was well past midnight before the French recaptured the ground they had lost and the attack was finally subdued. At dawn, groups of Turks were seen retiring and we helped them on their way. As the day wore on the 'Hood' and 'Anson' battalions moved over to the extreme left and took up a position across the Gully Ravine.

Sunday, 2nd May

At ten o'clock on this beautiful morning whilst the wild birds were singing merrily, we fixed bayonets and advanced to attack and found that the Turkish firing squad were waiting for us. We thought that after the punishment we had given them during the night, that they had moved out – we were wrong. Machine-gun and shrapnel fire soon made us spread out as we continued to advance in short rushes for about four hundred yards until we were ordered to stop and dig in to obtain some shelter from the withering fire. Our advance temporarily halted; the 2nd Hampshires came up to reinforce us, looking as though they were on the parade ground, they were in such perfect alignment. The Turks increased their shrapnel fire and it was so heavy that we were all ordered to retire to our positions originally held.

With the exception of the one unopposed on the 27th April, I took part in all of those suicidal, frontal daylight attacks that were attempted during the campaign. These were on 2nd, 6th, 7th and 8th May when we were on loan to the French and under the command of General d'Amade. I was in the first line of the attack on 4th June when the 'Collingwood' battalion was annihilated coming up behind us and the rest of the 2nd Naval Brigade almost wiped out between noon and half-past twelve. Again on 12th July when working with the Divisional Engineers in the 52nd Sector, I was commandeered to carry ammunition to the hard-pressed men in the advanced position they had captured and remained in the forward line for a couple of days.

After the evacuation of Anzac and Suvla Bay on 20th December, those of us at Cape Helles were left holding the baby. I was at this time working as a sapper in the 8th Mining Company and had for some time been tunnelling down the left side of the Gully.

Sunday, 19th December

At the appointed time we broke into the Gully and the HLI of the 52nd Division rushed from the opening we had made but only succeeded in getting half-way across the bed of the Gully as a large redoubt in the centre held up any further progress. Immediately we began to tunnel underneath it and by Wednesday 29th December

General Paul standing by dug-outs and bivouacs in a gully at Cape Helles.

Gully Beach. The existence of Gully Ravine was not known at the time of landing.

all was ready; our mine blew the redoubt to smithereens enabling the Royal Scots Fusiliers to join up with our men on the other side of the Gully which at this point was a mass of barbed wire.

Saturday, 1st January 1916

The beginning of a New Year; it looks much the same as the old one, but shells instead of bells herald it in. With the rest of my team I spent the whole day and most of the night carrying tins of Ammonal from a dump to the galleries in the firing line not meeting a soul between the dump and the firing line. Each day we found trenches we had trudged along hundreds of times were now completely blocked. We had to find other routes, only to find they, too, were blocked later in the day. For some time now the men in the front line have observed periods of silence during the hours of darkness, from one hour or more varying from day to day. During the daytime there is plenty of activity on the beaches and in the line but there appears to be no one in between. The French left on New Year's Day and I have not seen any of the 42nd Division lately.

Monday, 3rd January

We were told officially that Anzac and Suvla Bay had been evacuated but Cape Helles was to be held. In a deserted trench I found a notice saying that the 8th Army Corps would be relieved by the 9th Army Corps and to inform all concerned.

Friday, 7th January

At about eleven o'clock in the morning, the Turks began an intensive bombardment on both sides of the Gully. It was obvious that it was a prelude to an attack. The question was: 'How long have we to wait?'

As the hours passed, thousands of shells crashed into the empty support trenches and those that fell in the firing line took their toll. It was by far the most heaviest shelling I had experienced. At about 3 p.m. it was further intensified and at 3.30 p.m. there was a terrific crash followed by yet another upheaval – two mines had gone up.

Now came the expected attack. The Turks charged towards us shouting wildly. They had about a hundred yards to cover before reaching my particular part of the line though they had much less ground to cover a little further to the left. After their four and a half hours' warning, we were ready for them. There was no doubt in our minds that it was their intention to drive us over the cliffs close behind us.

Now that Anzac and Suvla Bay had been evacuated we were outnumbered by at least five to one; they came forward in their hundreds, some carrying timber for use in bridging our trenches. Perhaps they thought that after so many hours of concentrated shelling there would be no one to stop them, but they had not reckoned with the Staffordshires of the 13th Division and eight sappers who could handle a rifle as well as the rest. We should be able to – we had had plenty of practice. We blazed away at the advancing Turks who did not now appear to be in such a hurry to get to the coast. Some were becoming a little hesitant, but our warships standing close in helped them to make up their minds. I thought the Navy had deserted us long ago and it was very heartening to see and hear their salvos. We certainly needed their help. Our resident squibs are few and far between nowadays but no doubt they do their little best and a good little best at that.

As the sun went down behind us and into the eyes of the Turks, the attack petered out. I do not know the exact time as my faithful watch had been knocked about a bit but at a guess I would say roughly 6 p.m. The battle was over and the drive to the sea had ended where it had begun. Intermittent shell and rifle fire persisted but though there was considerable activity near the Turkish lines throughout the night, no further attempt was made on our positions. They were collecting their dead and wounded no doubt; they must have suffered enormous losses. So long as they restricted their movements to the region of their wire we did not disturb them. We had beaten them again but we knew they had plenty of reserves now that we had given up our other bridgeheads. They would come again with fresh troops, we did not expect any rest, nor did we get much. Throughout the night we were alternatively on the look-out on the fire-step for one hour on and trying to sleep the next and so on. Everyone was too keyed up to sleep though, we did not want to be caught napping at this late hour.

Saturday, 8th January

After a cool night the dawn reminded me of the long-gone spring dawns when I loved to roam among the heather. The air was so refreshing as the sun rose over the hills causing the mist in the valley to float away. The serenity enchanted me; the war seemed far away and hatred and strife non-existent – a world of peace and good-will. I was glad to be alive and wanted to stay that way, yet I knew this would be very difficult. Yesterday was Hell; what would today bring?

We thought today is 'Z' day, the day of our intended departure but this depended upon many things. Firstly, the guns must go, then the horses, then the mules. After these the supporting troops must all have left before the firing line is given up. Only a specified number can be evacuated during the hours of darkness. The trawlers and lighters must make many trips full to capacity and must leave at the appointed time to enable them to return for more. If we were to get away the sea must be reasonably calm, more than a slight swell would tear away the pontoons and our chances of leaving would go with them. Now there were only the remnants of four divisions left on the Peninsula, about 16,000 tired and weary men, half of them in the firing line, the others holding the last line of defence known to us as the 'Eski' line just inland from the beaches.

We do not know who is to remain to the end. Maybe there may be competition on the beaches as to who shall be the last to leave, but we have over three miles to walk after leaving the firing line; two and a half hours' journey providing there is no interruption. We must all await our turn. To those who have already left the forward zone and to those about to leave, we wish them the best of luck. We know we cannot all leave together as there are not enough small boats. The beaches are always shelled at night and, if the Turks became aware that we are leaving, every gun on the Peninsula and on the Asiatic side – and they have plenty – will be trained on the rickety embarkation piers and the barges alongside.

We have been told that the withdrawal from Anzac and Suvla Bay was carried out without the loss of a single man; maybe we too, will slip away unnoticed in the darkness though the element of surprise must have gone. Perhaps the Turks will be thankful we are leaving but, it would be a great boost to their morale if they were able to say that they threw us into the sea with heavy loss of men and matériel instead of having to admit they had been fooled for a second time within a month. These are my own thoughts. We do not discuss evacuation at this late hour but we know in our own hearts the odds are stacked against us all getting away. After the beating we gave them yesterday, they may have second thoughts about our leaving at the moment. In the front line we have only one thought – self-preservation. Each of us firmly believes he has the right to live but we will not shirk our responsibilities. Dusk is upon us and we, eight sappers, were ordered to unload the bullet in the breech. I took a parting shot at the enemy and strange to say, not really in anger but, with that bullet went all my cherished hopes. I had hoped that when my turn to leave this awful place came, I would walk with my head held high but it was not to be. With the breech of my rifle empty but the magazine full, I returned with the rest of my team to our advanced base at Geoghegan's Bluff to await further orders. We were issued with 'iron' rations for one day.

The waning moon had set as we began on our way across the Peninsula, our feet swathed with sandbags to muffle our footfalls. About an hour's walk through the lonely and deserted support trenches brought us to the Krithia road so well known to us. It was difficult to define exactly where we were but I think we had come along the trench known to us as Wigan road and had halted where it cut across 'B' Avenue. Here we were issued with a short strip of bandage to be worn on the arm to facilitate counting at the control points on the way down. After a while, we joined on the tail end of a party from the firing line and went on our way towards the beach. As we slowly tramped through the mud, a foot deep in many places, weary and tired, I could not believe we were leaving. I expected every moment to be ordered to 'about turn'. It was a long while since I had closed my eyes for more than a few brief moments but the thought of a remote chance of living kept me awake; each painful step was a foot nearer to freedom but, there are many steps in three miles. As we halted at the control points I instantly fell asleep, instinct waking me when the party moved off. We were all

(*Left*) Myself with the War Graves Commissioner standing on the front line at Gallipoli in 1934. (*Below*) V Beach at Sedd-el-Bahr.

the same – walking aimlessly and in a stupor.

A cool breeze brought my slumbers to an end; we were in the open a long way from the firing line and approaching 'V' beach. The moon had set a long time ago, it was very dark and strangely quiet. No one had time for words, we were all living in the past, the future did not exist any more – it was so far away and the past so near, so fresh in our minds. I imagined all my pals were with me as they had been on the day we landed, we were a motley crowd then, full of hope and anxious to do our best for Britain. Before we landed our Colonel had told us the eyes of the world would be upon us. The eyes of the Turks certainly were but the rest of the world had forgotten us. Maybe in the years to come they will remember but it will be much too late. The battle is over and the time for us to leave has arrived. The sole survivor of my section, I went wearily on my way to the beach leaving the bodies of my pals to enrich Turkish soil; I hope they will understand.

The pace quickened a little as we were behind schedule. As we climbed the gradual slope towards the cliffs, we heard the bugler on the fort at Sedd-ul-Bahr sound the long 'G'. He had observed the flash of the firing of 'Asiatic Annie'. We had twenty-eight seconds to take cover but as we were in the open there was nowhere to shelter. We plodded forward towards where we knew the shell, probably aimed at the beach, would land. With a resounding thud it fell directly ahead of us over the brow of the hill. If the shelling was of the usual type we should reach the shelter of the cliffs before the next shell arrived. When we finally arrived at the cliffs we sat waiting our turn to leave this inhospitable graveyard.

The bugler again sounded his warning note and more weary men came to the foot of the cliffs thinking it might be safer there. The shell fell close to the rickety pier and hurrying ghostly figures disappeared in the darkness, there was another warning note and another crash; more hurrying figures and more waiting. It was past midnight when my party were ordered to make for the pier and to board an iron lighter under the lee of the *River Clyde*. There was a heavy swell running and we went below with difficulty.

It was so crammed with men that it was impossible to raise one's hand to stifle a sneeze. The stench was overpowering; some men were sick, some fainted but could not fall and many were fast asleep – in spite of the historic occasion. No others came aboard; there was not room for even one more but still we waited.

Asiatic Annie, the gun we had laughed at hundreds of times, was now less of a joke. She was a menace and was threatening our escape. Imprisoned in this iron tomb we were so helpless, so near to escape and yet so close to death. The lighter rolled as another shell struck the water; the rolling increased considerably as a mass of exhausted humanity left the shore they could not see; a load of garbage to be dumped somewhere and forgotten. Perhaps as the years roll by they will be remembered as the expedition that was betrayed by jealousy, spite and indecision.

The Turks did not beat us – we were beaten by our own High Command.

CHAPTER THREE

We Join the Army

Lemnos: Sunday, 9th January 1916

The battalion re-assembled under canvas; a very motley crowd indeed. At first glance it was a happy crowd; happy to have survived the ordeal of a deserted army; an army that no-one wanted; an army that was denied everything except its own courage, an army that had fought its way up the cliffs to capture a foothold and had held the Turks for 259 days in spite of every conceivable obstacle placed in its way. A battered army but still unbeaten, mighty in the field of battle but a mere pawn in the field of politicians, to be pushed about and eventually sacrificed and forgotten.

The Gallipoli venture had failed; we had slipped away in the darkness. The evacuators had estimated that we would lose at least half of the 120,000 men (some of them only ten yards from the Turkish trenches) in doing so. Yet in face of this appalling prospect they recommended evacuation. Maybe because of the impending massacre all those who had advised evacuation had cleared out long before it began, leaving it to be carried out by the people who had always strongly opposed it.

Now it is all over. Early this morning I, and many others, were within rifle-fire of the Turks but now, thanks to the Royal Navy, there are 47 miles of sea between us, I can stand upright again without fear, I can move about quite freely but I cannot forget the chaps we left behind, many of them still unburied. I hope they will forgive us; we did not want to leave them even if it meant joining them in their everlasting vigil, custodians of a piece of barren land but enriched by the blood freely shed by the youth of the Empire. Throughout the ages great battles have been fought and many men have died in battle but I doubt if so many men have died in such a small area. The battlefield became a cemetery occupied by the living as well as the dead.

Monday, 10th January

Trying to put the jig-saw together again. I met men that I have not seen since disembarking from the *Grantully Castle* nearly nine months ago – goodness knows where they had been, others had been evacuated, sick or wounded, and had returned to the Peninsula when I wasn't looking. Some have had cushy base jobs and feel sorry for themselves at having lost such cushy numbers – they are very fit and well-dressed, I and lots of others are in rags – one lousy shirt, one pair of shorts that can stand up by themselves, also lousy; and a much battered Australian slouch hat with several bullet holes in it – that's how I came to acquire it. However I did manage a good pair of boots from a dump before I left – a few sizes too big but that is of no matter – nothing ever fits in the army. The most distracting thing is that I seem to take several steps before my feet leave the ground. Had the good old Navy ran short of boats I am positive I could have paddled my way here in my oversized boots.

I'm feeling better already and the weather is perfect. Rations are plentiful but there's not much assortment; the same old tack but somehow it seems to taste better, in fact everything seems better. The Chief Petty Officer's temper has mellowed and he seems to be a little shortsighted now. We are a real Fred Karno's army, or is it Navy? We can see the sea and smell the sea but that is our only connection with it. We are Naval ratings with Naval pay but sailors in name only; however that is of no consequential importance at the moment. We are out of the cage and on the wing – able to flutter in the breeze, able to stand up without fear – able to sit down away from the maggots – able to take a deep breath without feeling sick, able to sleep, to dream of home long since forgotten as a place of reality, with comfort and security I had failed to notice. It's good to be human again but there are times when it is painful. We do not

At Lemnos after the evacuation of Gallipoli on 9th January. Most of these men lost their lives in the fighting on the Ancre or Gavrelle in 1917. They were all of the late General Lord Freyberg's 'Hood' Battalion. I am fourth from the left in the row of those standing.

W Beach after the evacuation. Note the two traction engines.

talk of battles, we talk of our absent friends, enquiring of Bill and Taffy and Jock. We know the answer but we ask, we must ask. They were and still are, very dear to us; may they rest in peace. They will never be forgotten; their sacrifice enabled us survivors to live.

Saturday, 15th January

Very heavy rain prevented any parades. The whole day was spent trying to prevent the camp foundering and it got worse during the night. By morning the camp was under water. Nightfall – almost sunk, and still pouring down.

Monday, 17th January

Rumour has it that we are to garrison the island of Tenedos and the 2nd Naval Brigade are going to Salonica – we shall see.

Tuesday, 18th January

Issued with brand new uniforms and not before time. We do look smart and soldierly. Must keep it clean as we might get home leave.

Monday, 24th January

We began a march to the village of Thermos, about six miles so they say. Finished up following a goat track over the hills. It was the longest six miles I have ever marched but it had its compensation; we had a hot thermal bath, the first fresh water bath since leaving the transport in April last year, most refreshing.

Tuesday, 25th January

Now that we had been washed and ironed we were offered ten days leave at Malta. All the 'old hands' refused; we would wait for English leave!

Wednesday, 26th January

'Hawke' battalion left Lemnos for garrison duty on the island of Imbros. Getting close to the Peninsula again, less than twelve miles away.

Saturday, 29th January
First batch left for ten days leave at Malta. They were men of the 'Collingwood' and 'Benbow' battalions. It was to their advantage to accept the offer. We of the 'Hood' and 'Anson' battalions had left England on the last day of February but they had not sailed until the end of the first week in May.

Tuesday, 8th February
Up to now we have had a fairly easy time, a little drill, working parties doing all manner of things and nothing in particular but today we began to construct a rifle-range and, if I may say so, we did a good job. We must have done as we continued working at it for the rest of the week quite unmolested.

Sunday, 13th February
We vacated the tents and moved into huts that were once used as a hospital. They were very clean and tidy and we were told in no uncertain manner that we had to keep it that way. A great advantage on tents; we had somewhere to put our gear and be able to stretch out a bit. Unfortunately the nurses had gone.

Thursday, 17th February
My battalion seems to have disintegrated – some are supposed to have gone to garrison the island of Tenedos. Even my company, 'C', has been split; 1st and 2nd Platoons crossed the harbour to guard stores in East Mudros whilst the 3rd and 4th Platoons have taken over the village of Kastro as their base. Don't know what sort of a time they are having but it's miserable here in East Mudros, there's 'nowt' anywhere here, not even the stores we are supposed to be guarding.

Friday, 25th February
H.M.T. *Olympic* sailed into harbour with, some say, 10,000 troops aboard. As many of them were reinforcements for the Royal Naval Division, we would know soon. There was a strong rumour that she had arrived at the entrance of the harbour last night after closing-time. Apparently a boom is drawn across the entrance at a certain

hour to prevent 'strangers' and submarines from playing merry hell with the sitting ducks. It was said that while she was biding her time for sunrise, she had three torpedoes fired at her. True or false, rumours are our only information. She looked fine to me today; she's a real tonic.

Saturday, 26th February

Something in the wind. Every ship in the harbour had full steam up, the long and the tall, the short and the small, all the lot. Maybe we are going to evacuate the whole area and go home. What a hope!

Sunday, 27th February

HMT *Olympic* sailed out of the harbour carrying, so it was said, 38 officers and men from the 'Hood' battalion for a spot of leave in England. This is a hopeful sign; there are not many of the original battalion left so I should be included in the next batch. Wishful thinking maybe, but it is an awfully nice thought. Oh to be in England now that spring is here!

Friday, 3rd March

We were recalled to West Mudros and commenced field training at once, which meant that we marched here there and everywhere, skirmishing night and day with very little respite. We appeared to be getting ready for more combat duty somewhere.

Saturday, 11th March

We vacated the 27th General Hospital huts and took over the former Canadian Hospital. One large hut was taken over by the YMCA in the 'Nelson' lines. This proved to be a real blessing; we could sit at ease, chin-wagging to friends in our spare moments when not out on night operations in the hills and valleys.

Tuesday, 21st March

We left camp before daybreak for a four-day skirmish. Our venue was on the outskirts of the village of Thermos. The following day we were 'attacked' by the 'Nelson' battalion and forced to retire for about a mile and 'dug in'. They renewed their attack at dusk but, according to the umpires, we held our new positions.

Thursday, 23rd March

'Stood to arms' at 5.30 a.m. Battle appeared to be over at sunrise. We had physical drill for about an hour and then followed the goat tracks to Kastro and several other places. We were up before the larks again next day for more drill and range-finding. We were told that the battalion commander had agreed that the company that arrived back in camp first, in company formation and the least fatigued, would be excused first parade next morning. The very rough nature of the terrain caused the platoons to find their own goat-track. My platoon, the 1st, was the first to arrive in camp. We had to 'double up' to maintain our lead on the other three of 'C' company. The company's time was registered as one hour twenty minutes. We were carrying full pack of ninety pounds. I don't know how fatigued the rest of the battalion were; we certainly had had enough, but we had our morning off. We spent the whole of the next morning bathing in the sea.

Monday, 27th March

Took part in the consecration of the British cemetery at Portiarnos. After the solemn service the children attending gave us three rousing *Zetos*. (cheers)

Wednesday, 29th March and the following day

I spent the whole two days learning to handle a rifle at our newly made rifle-range and was quite pleased with myself having scored full possible marks, very much to my surprise! I was on parade in the late afternoon. All men of the original 'Hood' battalion that had landed on the Peninsula in April 1915 were ordered to take two paces forward; only fifteen of us stepped forward out of the nine hundred, who had not left the Peninsula during the whole campaign. We were 'told off' for English leave but no date was mentioned. Of the men on parade some had been months, some weeks and some only a few days before wounds or disease caused them to be evacuated to hospitals on Lemnos, Cyprus and Egypt; some had managed to get to England.

Sunday, 2nd April

Marched passed Sir A. Paris, GOC Royal Naval Division. In his short speech afterwards he told us that the division would soon be disbanded through no fault of our own.

Friday, 7th April

We marched passed Admiral de Robeck and General Sir A. Paris. The inspection by the Admiral was taken to mean that the Navy were about to hand us over to the ship-breakers. Where did we go from here? We were fully trained soldiers masquerading as sailors in name only with plenty of fighting experience behind us.

Saturday, 15th April

We were ordered to be in readiness to move off at twenty-four hours notice to fulfil a military operation, whatever that meant. There was a very strong rumour that we were to raid the Asia Minor coast to relieve the pressure on General Townshend besieged at Kut.

Tuesday, 18th April

The weather is still glorious – mornings and evenings quite cool and refreshing, mid-day very hot but bearable. As usual, we paid our weekly visit to the thermal baths at Thermos. It had become customary for us to parade in our shirt sleeves for these marches. The discarding of our heavy material tunics was much appreciated. Today was no exception and we set off full of the joys of spring – over the hills and down the dales, following the goat tracks wherever they chose to wander. We had covered about half of the six miles when it began to rain. For a while it was refreshing but it increased to a very heavy downpour and washed away all the joys long before we reached the warm, steaming bath-chamber with its shallow stone troughs overflowing on to the warm stone floor. A brisk rub down with a now very wet towel seemed to be purposeless as our shirts were still dripping wet and the rain showed no sign of abating until we had completed our return march to our camp. Thank goodness it was a warm rain.

Sunday, 23rd April

A year ago today, Rupert Brooke of 'A' company, 'Hood' battalion died from sunstroke and severe blood poisoning from the insect bite on his lip and was buried on the island of Scyros; during the days that followed many, many more men, young and old, died in battle less than fifty miles away. Try as I might, it was difficult to forget those we have left behind in those desolated places. I knew them so well. Today was St George's Day and I must turn my thoughts to the living. My pal Bill Howell has a brother on HMS *Cornwallis* which is lying in the harbour. We have had our request to visit him from 1.30 to 6.30 p.m. granted in writing. We boarded the picquet boat lying alongside the pier but instead of going to the *Cornwallis* we were dumped aboard her sister-ship, HMS *Russell* – they said they would call to take us to the *Cornwallis* later. The 'Pukka' sailors made a great fuss of us; a lovely tea, I hadn't seen such a lovely spread for donkey's years. Afterwards we swopped yarns. They were most interested in our experiences and we in theirs. If the picquet boat did call for us, and they said they did, well, we didn't hear them and stayed aboard the *Russell* until 6.30 p.m.

Tuesday, 25th April

The anniversary of the landing on the Peninsula. Officially it seemed to have been forgotten but it is, and always will be, remembered by the 'Old hands' who took part in it, unnoticed by the War correspondents, miles out to sea.

Wednesday, 26th April

Bad news always travels fast in any part of the world. We have been told that HMS *Russell* had been sunk by a submarine whilst waiting to enter Malta harbour. I hoped that those chaps that made my pal and me so welcome last Sunday were safe and well. They thought that our occupation was hazardous. In war, very few of those taking an active part in it are at any time out of danger on land or sea.

Sunday, 30th April
The circumstances of our visit to the *Russell* had been explained to Lieutenant Cockey who again gave us the very necessary permit to visit HMS *Cornwallis*. This time we managed to be put aboard the right vessel and were greeted by Bill's brother and his mess-mates. Not only had we had plenty to eat but we came away with a sackful of bread each which would of course be shared with our pals. Later that evening a party left for Stavros on the Salonica front to act as a working party, so they said. Could be that they are the advance party for the division!

Tuesday, 2nd May
We began practising landing from the transport with full pack and carrying either a pick or a shovel for good measure. We descended Jacob's ladder rather awkwardly into the ship's cutters, and rowed ourselves ashore; not only once as we were kept at it all day and for the rest of the week. Sometimes we would dig in just beyond the beach but the main purpose of the exercise appeared to be making sure that we had mastered the art of reaching the shore and be able to stand up when we reached the God-forsaken beach. As there was no restriction as to the amount of noise we made we were able to give vent to our feelings in the usual soldierly fashion and felt much better after getting it off our chests.

Sunday, 7th May
The 2nd Royal Marines and the 'Howe' battalion embarked on the *Empress of Britain* bound for Marseilles. This is understood to mean that the division will end up on the Western Front. The scattered flock will have to be gathered in, for at the moment units of the division are dispersed all over the Mediterranean, the working party on the Salonica front, the 'Anson' battalion doing garrison duty at Alexandria and the 'Hawke' battalion on the same mission on Imbros. Some of the 'Hood' battalion are in Tenedos, and goodness knows where the rest of them are at this moment. All this landing from open boats we have been practising of late will be of no earthly use on the Western Front.

Saturday, 13th May
'Hood' battalion held their own sports on the only flat piece of ground on the island. This occasion was welcomed by all, not so much for taking part in the numerous events but as a relief from the monotonous drilling. We felt quite human once more. In the evening the 'Anson' battalion arrived from Alexandria. The gathering of the clan is rapidly taking shape. Now it seems certain we are ear-marked for France.

Tuesday, 16th May
'Hood' and 'Nelson' battalions embarked on the *Ivonion* and sailed at once for Marseilles. Goodbye to the mystic Middle East, to me a tragic Middle East, brimful of many painful memories that disturb my thoughts throughout the day as well as the night. Try as I may, and my God I do try, I cannot forget the slaughter of so many of my pals who set out with me on this mission, so full of hope. Many of them lie unburied on that desolate scrubland. Nor can I free my nostrils of that stench that permeated the Peninsula.

Sunday, 21st May
We arrived at Marseilles at eight o'clock in the evening after an uneventful voyage apart from many rumours and consequent counter-action. The Aegean, Ionian and Mediterranean seas seem to be infested by submarines, or was the 'look-out' mistaking them for the friendly porpoises bent on escorting us.

As usual, within an hour, 'C' company was on the dock-side as a working party throwing baggage about until the early hours of the morning. After five days at sea it was a nice change to feel the good earth again. Cobblestones don't pitch and roll – well, not so much as the old tub we arrived in did.

Monday, 22nd May
We disembarked from the *Ivonian* at 4 p.m. After roughly an hour's march through the crowded streets and a rousing welcome, we boarded the train that would be our home for the next couple of days. The march through the town in daylight with our bandsmen blowing their heads off made us feel quite important and if I may say so, very proud.

Many months ago we had left our camp at Blandford on a dark and rainy night and made our way across ploughed fields and muddy downs to avoid the roads, to a station miles away, in case the secret of our departure had leaked out. We sailed from Avonmouth with less than half-a-dozen on the dock-side to wave us 'Goodbye'; we arrived in and left Egypt unheralded; we sneaked ashore on the Gallipoli Peninsula and, after a terrible bashing, the few of us that were left sneaked away in the dark not bothering to say 'Goodbye' to our hosts for almost nine months. We did in our hearts say a quiet farewell to the many that were not able to leave with us.

Today things were very different. The reception committee at Gallipoli greeted us with rifles and jeers but the people of Marseilles greeted us with flags and cheers. At last, after travelling thousands of miles, we had found somewhere we appeared to be welcome. In case we overstayed our welcome we left at 5 p.m.

Tuesday, 23rd May

At eleven o'clock in the morning our train steamed into Lyons to another great welcome. French Red Cross nurses gave everyone quench-thirsting coffee and food and really made quite a respectable fuss of us. The train pulled out with most of my crowd hanging on the outside of the carriages.

Wednesday, 24th May

At breakfast time we were shunted into a siding of a large junction about eighteen kilometres south of Paris, so the natives said. After a good breakfast, the first hot meal since we left the transport at Marseilles, we left the PLM line, much to our dismay as we were looking forward to seeing Paris. Our journey from the Mediterranean had been a pleasant one; our pastime was writing messages with indelible pencil on the big hard biscuits we were supposed to eat and throwing them out on to the platforms of the stations we passed through. These messages informed the finder that now the Royal Naval Division had arrived in France, their worries were practically over. We would knock the Jerries out of France or would evacuate ourselves.

Now we were near the war zone the rest of our journey would be via branch lines. About noon we were diverted into a siding at another junction. There was war matériel everywhere and hundreds of French troops who, by their appearance, had been in the fighting area. After much amusing gesticulating on my part I gleaned that they had been in the Verdun sector and were out for a well-earned rest.

We detrained at seven o'clock a few miles from Abbeville at a small station called Pont Rémy. Tea was waiting for us when we arrived. It must have been waiting since we left Marseilles, as it was icy cold with neither milk or sugar – it was lousy. After marching in the pouring rain we arrived at the village of Citerne (Oise) and were billeted in old stables. This was to be our training area as all new arrivals in France, whether they had seen any active service or not, had to get acclimatised to the new conditions, before moving up in stages. There were a lot of other things we would have to get used to. We would be at times living among civilians, and after the day's toil we would be able to go to an *estaminet* for rum and coffee, or rum without the coffee if we had received our five francs pay. I like this village; everyone appears to be friendly, it was worth the ten kilometres march in the pouring rain from Pont Rémy.

Thursday, 25th May

We had the day to ourselves to sort ourselves out and we certainly needed sorting out. Last night we slept where we could; today we have been allocated to another stable, even more airy than last night's and our clothes are still wet and most uncomfortable, but the straw fire in the barn-yard is helping matters.

Friday, 26th May

Reveille, 6 a.m. Parade 6.30, Physical drill until 7 a.m. Breakfast 7.30. Battalion Parade 9 a.m. Full marching order, less blanket, for a route march until noon. Dismiss. Dinner, 12.30. Company parade, 2 p.m. Route march until 3.30. Tea, 4.30. Free for the rest of the day. Our battalion commander, Lieutenant-Commander Freyberg DSO was thrown from his horse and broke his arm in three places, so it was rumoured.

Sunday, 28th May
Three men from the 'Hood' granted English leave. Well, it's a start and I think I shall be in the next batch. I sincerely hope so.

Friday, 2nd June
Reorganization, whatever that means. We seemed to be reorganizing every month. 'A' and 'C' companies are to form the 1st 'Hood', 'B' and 'D' companies to form the 2nd 'Hood' battalions.

Sunday, 4th June
Another day of sad memories: the slaughter on Gallipoli. There were no parades so I took a look at the surrounding countryside. Hallencourt by way of Marelessart and then by the main road to Oisemont via Allery – a long but pleasant stroll.

Tuesday, 6th June
After the usual ceremony of hoisting the White Ensign, we, the 1st 'Hood', went for our route march of arguable kilometres and on returning found the leave party that had left Mudros on the *Olympic* on 27th February had arrived from home. There had been so much uncertainty as to the destiny of the division, that their leave had been extended until such times as it was finally decided once and for all. Late that evening I was told that a draw had taken place and that my number was eighteen. On making further enquiries, I found that I was last out of the hat for leave; even so, there were only fifteen of the original 'Hoods' who were on parade on 29th March that had not left the Peninsula during the campaign. Three had gone on 28th May. I don't understand the Navy's arithmetic but there is nothing I can do.

Friday, 9th June
Night operations in the Hallencourt area. Here, there and everywhere.

Saturday, 10th June
We had our first taste of gas – we had to walk through a cloud of

lachrymatory gas much stronger than we would be subjected to up the line. I have never felt so sorry for myself in my whole life, nor have I shed so many tears.

Saturday, 17th June

We appear to have finished our training in the 'back area'. At midnight we left Citerne and marched to Abbeville arriving at 5 a.m. and boarding the train at 8.30 a.m. After a five-hour journey which included many shuntings and stops we detrained at Bruay. A march of about eighteen kilometres brought us to the village of Dieval, roughly mid-way between Bruay and St Pol. We were billeted in old barns and stables as usual and shared them with an old cow or two.

CHAPTER FOUR

Learning the Lewis Gun

Wednesday, 21st June

Now we are under the Army we must alter our style of bayonet fighting. Up to now the Navy stance has been used and considered very efficient; well I'm still alive, but now it is out. Instead of bending knees in a sitting stance, we must bend the left knee only, the right leg must be rigid and the body leaned forward with the weight on the left leg. The point of the bayonet will be a foot nearer to the enemy than it was with the old naval style, provided of course he is coming towards you and you are waiting for him to oblige. However, all this week we have been moving forward towards a sack of straw suspended between two poles and thrusting the bayonet right home without the slightest opposition from the lifeless sack. 'To withdraw the bayonet from its bloody position, the right hand is brought forward beyond the left hand to give you more purchase', in other words, a shorter hold, so said the instructor who had never heard a shell burst and the only enemy he had seen was behind barbed wire in a prisoners' cage. Of course it is much easier and quicker to put your foot on the victim's stomach but the instructor would not know that.

Sunday, 25th June

We were inspected by the GOC 4th Army Corps. This is the usual practice. The General takes the opportunity of seeing his troops before he commits them to the slaughterhouse. He won't be coming with us as he is much too important to take any personal risk. He will conduct the operations from a far-off château in the rear surrounded by maps and countless staff officers with their batmen. The ground gained, if any, will be measured in yards, not in lives.

Wednesday, 28th June
We left Dieval at nine o'clock in the morning and marched to Hersin Coupigny arriving there just before six-thirty in the evening. We are on our way to the battle zone and apparently there is no time to lose for at ten o'clock on the following morning we were on the move again arriving at Villers-au-Bois in the Vimy Ridge section.

Friday, 30th June
We have had our baptism of fire on the Western Front. For several days the artillery have been bombarding the whole area. Our job tonight was to dig a cable trench on the Ridge about a hundred yards behind the front line. Even before we got into position out in the open, the Germans were spraying the whole of the back area with shrapnel. As the night wore on it became impossible to remain any longer in the open and we were withdrawn to the shelter in a nearby trench which seemed to me to be their target. The incessant bursting shrapnel turned the darkness into light. It had a likewise effect on my hair, I think.

Sunday, 2nd July
For the third night we were digging on the Ridge and subjected to more than the usual shell-fire. The terrific cannonade on our right that has been going on night and day for more than a week now seems to have spread towards us for during the night the shelling was intensified. Away over in the low lying ground on our left the British were sending clouds of gas that drifted slowly towards Lens. The Germans were placing what appeared to be fire buckets on their parapets in an attempt to cause the gas to rise. The artillery and the trench mortars soon put an end to their usefulness, if they were in fact, of any use.

Tuesday, 4th July
The 'Londons' holding the line in front of us livened up the night by a bombing raid and we got the backwash. Fortunately, most of the bullets sang their way overhead. They say these bombing raids are

commonplace; the idea is to capture a prisoner so that we know what regiment is opposing us at any given moment. As the raids take place along the whole front, those nicely polished brass-hats in their comfortable château well out of range, can deduce the movements of the enemy. This information, I agree, is vital but by the time it is collated it will be as much use as the corpses left out in the open as the result of the raid.

Wednesday, 5th July
We left Villers-au-Bois and eventually settled down in the village of Verdrel. The following day the newly created 2nd 'Hood' was disbanded. 'B' and 'D' Companies that formed it rejoined the original battalion.

Monday, 10th July
We left Verdrel and marched to Coupigny. After about an hour's rest, dinner was served by the roadside – the usual bully-beef stew – ghastly stuff. I shall never get to enjoying the beastly stuff. I swallowed the insipid stuff as there was no other choice, and, what makes it worse, the cooks never go into the front line. They would not last long if they did; but it isn't their fault entirely, they can only cook what is given them. Fully refreshed after such a sumptuous meal, we marched on to Bully-Grenay. We cannot get away from bully! The place is in ruins but there are quite a few civilians still about in spite of the constant shelling. Tea was doled out before we entered the communication trench that begins amongst the ruins. This trench is the only way we can reach the front line of the sector known to us as the Morocco Sector with the town of Lens immediately in front. We are here to have 'instructions' on how they fight the war in France and, of course, we have all the donkey work to do; but as far as we are concerned, we don't need any instructing; we are past masters of that act, and of dodging it also. If a soldier did all the work allocated to him he would never reach the firing line; he would have perished from sheer exhaustion. Morale must be maintained – keep him busy always so that he is much too tired to understand anything.

The famous Hanging Virgin on the church at Albert. Legend had it that when she fell the war would end.

Friday, 14th July
We were relieved by the 1st Royal Marines and marched back to Coupigny. Our brief stay here on our way up the line was by the roadside but tonight we seemed to be making preparations for a longer stay. Shattered barns and stables give us shelter from the icy cold wind but not from the pouring rain as the roofs are missing. Anywhere in the rear is an improvement on the firing line, however bad the conditions. One can sleep; one *must* sleep if not working as it may be days before you get another chance of a little shut-eye.

Sunday, 16th July
We left Coupigny at 10 p.m. and marched to Bouvigny Woods. We were billeted in huts which gave us the chance to dry out as it came down in torrents during the whole of our march. I wonder if it rains all the time in France – it seems so.

Wednesday, 19th July
We vacated the huts and took over the firing line – Northumberland Avenue and Kellet line. The sector seems very quiet but a little to the right, Vimy Ridge is always lively. Our positions are in Souchez Valley. We refer to it as 'Death Valley'. There are trenches everywhere, most of them apparently long since abandoned. At night we occupy one of these, but withdraw before daylight, leaving a patrol to hold part of a particular trench. There are seven men in my patrol occupying a detached post during the hours of daylight. Because of the extremely exposed nature of the valley which is dominated by Vimy Ridge, we have to lie low and exist on 'hard tack'; any movement would be fatal. If the Germans attacked we, if we survived, would certainly be captured. Our main defence line is on Lorette Spur behind us, but there is a lot of ground to be covered before reaching the Spur.

Wednesday, 26th July
Our spell in the firing line is completed. We were relieved by the 'Drake' battalion and came back to Aix-Noulette on the Arras-Béthune road roughly mid-way between these two towns. Although

this road is within easy range of the enemy, there is considerable traffic on it by day as well as night and in consequence it is always shelled. Aix-Noulette, in common with all the other villages in this area is in ruins. The church that stood upon the corner of the cross-roads, is only a shell, yet the crucifix is untouched as it hangs upon the almost completely shattered wall. It gave me cause for meditation as I gazed at it among the ruins and desolation.

Monday, 31st July

Each and every night since we were relieved by the 'Drakes', we have been back up the line as working parties, digging new trenches or repairing those that had offended Jerry during the day, carrying rations or material from one dump to another, sometimes walking aimlessly throughout the night without doing any actual work having repeatedly taken the wrong turning. There was no fear of taking the wrong turning tonight as we were to relieve the 'Drakes' in the firing. Other crowds seem to make a point of getting lost on their way to the line but not us, even though we are always half asleep and walk most of the way with our eyes closed until rudely awakened when we trip over one of the thousands of signal wires that run in every direction in every communication trench, or so it would seem. We don't waste time in the front line; we continue into 'No man's land' to take up our outpost positions in the valley, hoping that, when the time comes for us to retire to the front line somewhere in the near future, (no one ever knows within a day or so, or if they do they never tell us) we shall be able to find it and have something warm to eat and drink. There is nothing warm to be had here, except the enemy's fire if you show the least sign of movement. In the isolation of outpost duty, the war becomes a private affair consisting of groups of half-a-dozen out of touch with other groups, out of touch with the men in the front line. Out of sight, out of mind seems to be the official attitude. But I must admit outpost duty has its advantages. To be left alone for a little while with no one telling you what to do and then complaining about the way you do it, is wonderful. Out of the line if you are not hard at work you must be dodging the column and can expect a dressing down if any of the 'line dodging wallahs' catch you. Here is peace, perfect peace if the shelling has impaired your hearing and paralysed your brain.

Sunday, 6th August

We were relieved from the Valley by the 'Drake' battalion and take over the support line on the Lorette Spur known as the 'Dug-out line'. Considering that this ridge must be the gateway to the west as it was captured by the French way back in 1915 at a frightful cost, the defences are of a most casual order. They must have been dug under constant fire from Vimy Ridge which dominates the whole area. No attempt seems to have been made to improve them in any way; they are shallow and very exposed. How the French managed to capture this Spur is a mystery to me and how we manage to hold on to it is even a bigger mystery. On the forward slope the trenches are quite useless and of no depth and on the other side there are no trenches at all. There are no earthworks or troops for miles, the area is wide open. When we are not in the front line we are supposed to be in support. Each and every night we vacate this line and proceed up to the firing line and beyond it into the valley in isolated working parties. Sometimes during the night we see other parties wandering about but we don't know who they are. They could be our own men but they could be German patrols. No one knows or cares. We get on with the job in hand and leave it at that.

Thursday, 10th August

Another of our aeroplanes was brought down in the German lines whilst flying very low. This is the third to be lost in the last four days – three in the enemy lines and one in ours. This one disintegrated as it fell, quite close to us.

Saturday, 12th August

Our artillery have bombarded Vimy Ridge for half-an-hour and we get the backwash as usual, quite a few directs hits on our lines. This tit-for-tat shelling seems to be a waste of men and ammunition. During the night we were relieved from 'South Alley' (Dug-out line) and made our way back to Bouvigny-Boyeffles.

Sunday, 20th August

Yesterday I was 'told off' to go for a course of Lewis gun instruction and arrived overnight at Hersin-Coupigny, and slept in a ditch. This morning, after a lot of mucking about, I was given a bus ride to Béthune, a nice change from walking; my first ride anywhere and no conductor to demand my fare. It was a bit bumpy but I enjoyed the ride, much better than Shanks' pony. I boarded a train and went full pelt as far as St Pol then, after waiting for six hours stranded in a siding as usual, we eventually moved out and arrived at Etaples very late in the evening. An hour's march brought us to our destination, the Lewis gun school at Paris-Plage. The organization here is perfect in every detail. There were tents in perfect lines with plenty of room to move about and not too crowded. In a matter of minutes everyone knew the layout of the school, where he washed, dined and slept, his instructor and the routine in general. Reveille at 5.30 a.m. Physical drill parade 7 to 8 a.m. then breakfast. Parade for instruction at 9 a.m. to 1 p.m. then dinner. Afternoon parade at 2 o'clock until 4.15 then tea; the rest of the day free to do whatever we wished. I know I am going to enjoy my stay here although I have never seen a Lewis gun, let alone fired one.

Monday, 21st August

After a good night's rest, the first for a very long time, I didn't mind beating the larks on the golf course. Running around gave me a hearty appetite for breakfast and jolly nice it was – bacon that put up no resistance when I stuck my fork in it, real fresh bread and plenty of unboiled tea to wash it down. What more could a fighting man wish for? Casual enquiries told me that most of the men in my team have at least some knowledge of the Lewis Gun and some have even fired one. I realized that I should have to pull up my socks to keep in line with the class. As this was our first day at school we paraded a little before 9 a.m. Our instructor detailed one man to collect the gun from the armoury and to take it to our table already in position in a straight line on the flat sandy ground immediately in front of our tents.

At exactly nine o'clock our instructor blew his whistle. The school had commenced. We covered the intervening fifty yards at the double and at another blast from his whistle the class was seated on the forms feeling as playful as schoolboys on the last day of term. There are many such classes; the sergeant-instructors are all drawn from the Artists' Rifles and certainly know their drill and, what is more essential, they know how to teach. Above all, they are human and very considerate. I rather envy their smart rig-outs, trousers neatly creased, buttons and boots glistening in the bright sunlight. In comparison, the class are a shabby looking lot. The day before we had all been in the forward trenches. Personally, I have not had time to repair a rather large tear in the seat of my trousers, nor has the ugly barbed-wire scratch on my posterior healed; it is still very sore which accounts for my slowness in obeying the instructor's first order, to get seated comfortably before he began teaching. When the whistle sounded at the end of the morning session I had a general idea of the history of the gun and how it functioned and felt confident that I would be able to master it before the end of the course under such expert teaching.

After a good dinner we paraded at two o'clock. It was the same procedure as in the morning; the whistle and the fifty yard sprint. Each man had to take his turn in dismantling or assembling the gun according to the progress of the instruction. By the end of the day we all had had several go's and had the feel of it. I am now certain I will not be at the bottom of the class on the day of reckoning. It is my turn to bring the gun to the table tomorrow.

After a substantial tea the rest of the evening was free. Paris-Plage was only about a mile distant and Etaples was also within walking distance. The whole of my class with one exception – an old soldier who had a son older than I – had flitted away to sample the wine, women and song in the nearby habitation. The thought of my ambling among the civilians with the seat of my trousers flapping in the cool breeze did not appeal to me. There may be in the evenings that lie ahead ample time to go visiting. I know there are many reinforcements for the Royal Naval Division at Etaples, most of them having recovered from their wounds are now officially deemed to be ready to face the slaughter again as soon as they can be entrained to the battle area. For the moment I had to get on with

Two of my section with a Lewis gun.

my mending; my strictly limited length of string had to be teased out, much to the amusement of my companion whose brogue left no doubt as to his connection with the leprechauns. My marlin-spike, part of my Naval kit, served as a needle and after much effort the job was completed to my intense satisfaction. Now I was fully dressed, respectable and much more comfortable. There was still no sign of the happy warriors though it was getting rather late; in fact I think we two were the only people in the whole camp. Our conversation veered round to the intricacies of the Lewis gun and his apparent knowledge of it astounded me. To me, he knew all there was to know. I wondered why he was taking the course and told him so.

'Well now, my boy, I am a little surprised myself. I think the Colonel must have thought I needed a change from the firing line.'

'If I had your knowledge I would have a shot at becoming an instructor.'

'To be an instructor me boy, you have to be able to quote from the book like a parrot; you know the stuff I mean. "To load the gun you take a magazine of 47 rounds and place it on the magazine-post, thus. To fire the gun, rotate the magazine, pull back the cocking handle," and so on. You know the drill, me boy. That's what I've been trying to do all this evening while you were doing your trouser mending.'

He showed me the book of instructions he had borrowed, or maybe pinched, suggesting that we could help each other and admitting that reading was not his strong point. We began our lessons there and then. I read a page very slowly and he repeated every word, parrot fashion. Not until we had mastered the first page did we move on to the next. At first it was extremely interesting but as time went on, it became increasingly boring though I was intent on mastering the gun before the week's course had ended.

During the subsequent days 'in class' the knowledge I had gained was most helpful. I was able to strip and re-assemble the gun with ease, moreover I knew exactly the precise function of every single part. Every day an officer made his rounds, he would stand a few yards away from the class reading what looked like the instruction book to me before coming forward. I made it my business to be in possession of the gun when he approached the class. His routine was the same every time he came to the class, he would stand behind the man on the gun and, at the opportune moment, which would appear to coincide with the paragraph he had just read, he would very politely instruct him to be the instructor for the next few minutes. This suited my book perfectly as I was able to ramble on from memory. It made no difference to me whether I was at that moment stripping or re-assembling. I was able to demonstrate to the class with all the confidence in the world, much to his satisfaction, and my delight. As usual, he enquired my name and made the necessary note in his book.

Wednesday, 23rd August

After tea, Paddy and I made our way back to our tent but our hopes of continuing our lessons alone was not to be, as everyone had decided to stay in camp. It had to come sooner or later as the precious few francs they had could not last more than one glorious night on the razzle. Pay-days are by no means regular; in fact they are most irregular. Naturally one is never paid whilst in the forward zone which was quite understandable, but it didn't follow that we received the back money when the next pay-day came. Oh no, what was due had apparently no bearing on what you received. Occasionally we receive the handsome sum of ten francs each but the usual payment for the blood and sweat we had given is five francs and that is not very often, but we manage – we have to. At the moment money is of no concern; the food is excellent and the lodging free, the weather almost perfect and the open-air school interesting.

I was feeling very confident that I would pass the test at the end of the term but I realised there was still much to learn and with this in mind, I suggested to Paddy that we might take a walk away from the madding crowd. We strolled at ease over the golf links towards Paris-Plage, reciting our little pieces each trying to catch the other out and sometimes succeeding. We gave ourselves a break when we reached the town and had a drink on each other but we resumed our lessons quite seriously on our way back to camp. The only distraction came from the officers and their nurses from the nearby hospital for shell-shocked cases. From my personal observations I was much more shocked than the officers but it was not shell-shock. The following night we altered course and made our way to Etaples.

Although I mingled freely with the Royal Naval Division reinforcements I did not find anyone I knew; we old sweats seem to be getting rare. Paddy ferreted out one of his pals who had settled himself quite nicely in a staff job that carried the rank of sergeant. His job was to round up the lost sheep that had strayed from the pen and to make certain that they didn't stray again; they were needed in the battle zone, not in Etaples. There were plenty of 'specialists' here already and they had no intention of being replaced by real soldiers. These 'Camp-Wallahs' were having a nice, quiet and comfortable war and they knew it; they were better off than they were at home. I must, however admit that Paddy's pal had seen his share of mud and slaughter in the fighting zone. Fellow feeling is wondrously kind; he treated us with honours in the sergeants' mess. We stayed rather late and quaffed rather more red wine than we were accustomed to of late. The way back to the school seemed longer and much less straight than we had noticed on the way out and teaching was forgotten. My mind was muddled and my vision hazy, time and time again I had to pick myself up from the cold, cold ground. On one occasion I met Paddy coming towards me; even in my dazed condition I knew that one of us must be in error as we had left Etaples arm-in-arm and should be still going in the same direction. There was only one thing to do so we sat down to figure out the right course, we must have fallen asleep, for how long I have no idea; the cold brought us to our senses and we arrived back in camp very late, or was it very early?

Friday, 25th August

We had our final instruction which lasted the whole of the forenoon. We were supposed to know all there is to know; how to strip and re-assemble, how to clear the usual three stoppages indicated by the position of the cocking handle and so on. The afternoon was spent at the firing range and what amazed me most was the liveliness of the gun. The experts could, and did, fire a single round but however much I tried I could not fire less than at least ten and I thought I had a delicate touch – my goodness, this is a deadly toy, so light and easy to handle.

Saturday, 26th August

Paraded outside a marquee and, after quite some time, I was ushered inside and interviewed by whom I believed to be the Camp Commandant, a charming fellow. He asked many questions – regiment, division, how long had I been in France, where I had served before coming to the Western Front etc. On being told Egypt and Gallipoli he was most interested: did I find any difference in the fighting on the different fronts?

'It doesn't seem the same war to me. We have been here for more than three months and have not seen any real fighting by the Infantry.' On Gallipoli it was almost continuous fighting; the trenches were so close to each other, only ten yards apart in many cases, we relied on the infantryman's rifle and bayonet, whereas out here the trenches are so far apart that one seldom uses his rifle. The coloured lights go up if any movement is observed in 'No man's land' and the artillery deal with the situation. On Gallipoli any movement out in front would mean hand-to-hand combat to hold on to our trench or to capture the enemy's, and be quite sharp about it. Out here one seemed to have all the time in the world to take aim, moreover the trenches are very thinly manned as everyone is either digging or engaged in working parties carrying stuff about. I have yet to see my first German and dread to think what would happen if they decided to attack. The men in support are never really in support at all; they are scattered about here, there and everywhere doing all sorts of jobs and so detached as to render them useless as a fighting force in case of a surprise attack. The reserves, if any, are not within miles of the front line. I know of course, with the advent of such a concentration of artillery the infantryman has a very small part to play but he is nevertheless indispensable. 'Of course I can speak only of my own sector; what the position is on the other sectors I have no idea but they could not be more vulnerable.'

'You appear to be a very observant young man and your instructor is in no doubt as to your ability with the Lewis Gun. Will you please assemble the bits and pieces you see before you on the table – take your time.'

In less than a minute I had the gun assembled.

'Very good indeed. Now strip the gun and explain the parts and their uses as you go along.'

I had spent every spare moment of the last week doing just this according to the book. I felt very confident and had no difficulty in obeying the order; it was so easy.

'That was excellent. Would you like to be an instructor?'

'To be anything in Paris-Plage would be Heaven in comparison to the Hell I'm used to!' I said with a cheeky smile, which was returned.

The interview was over and I knew I had passed with flying colours.

CHAPTER FIVE

Back to the Front

Sunday, 27th August

The holiday is over. We left the school and marched to the camp at Etaples arriving at 7 p.m. Not allowed out. I said good-bye to Paddy and thanked him. We repeatedly 'fell in' and repeatedly 'fell out'. The party is slowly decreasing in numbers and in spirit. It's like waiting for execution – a few lonely souls among an army of 'Camp Wallahs' who treat us as though we have the plague. I really long to be back in the forward area amongst my own class, where men understand each other's feelings and know what it is all about, where strangers meet strangers and they are no longer strangers – a communion of spirit. The sun sets, the moon and the stars are obliterated by the foul smoke of the never-ending bombardment, yet there is light, radiant light that warms us all and gives us a sense of security. The pervading fear gives way to hope; a weed is a plant out of place, and in the forward area there is no real distinction, no classification – a weed is as exotic as an orchid. There is a wonderful feeling of comradeship among the lads in the line. No one knows who will be the next to bid farewell to all that he dearly cherishes, yet everyone believes in his heart that it will be himself.

There are times, yes many times, when each and every one of us would welcome the relief from this torment. It is not cowardice – far from it. It could be bravery. After all is said and done, bravery and cowardice are blood relations; there is a touch of insanity in both. It's only a question of degree and who is competent to judge? Show me the man who has never felt the pangs of fear. I have seen the bravest of men cowering and I have seen cowering men rise and go forward and even give encouragement to others. Fear will make you bury your head in the mud or shelter behind a blade of grass; it will make you run forward without rhyme or reason or it may completely immobilise you; it is unpredictable. Under prolonged stress the brain becomes fuddled, the power of reasoning is not there any more; it ceases to control the body and thoughts and movements are irrational. Even the vision is impaired and the soul tarnished. War overrules civilization and plunges humanity back thousands of years. We revert to being wild animals and the law of the jungle predominates; kill or be killed. Yet, away from the holocaust for a few days, we appear to regain our sanity, we act normally, but do we, will we ever, become normal again? We may mask our feelings, our bodily wounds may heal, our scars grow fainter with the passage of time, our speech again rational; we will forget the names of men and places but we shall never forget the slaughter of the young, and of the old, of our generation.

Monday, 28th August

After standing about in the rain for an hour or so, we boarded the train at 4 a.m. and left Etaples almost at once. This was most unusual and gave rise to many comments. They were glad to get rid of us or they couldn't carry on the real war without us? Whatever the reason we were on our way to the slaughter-house with almost indecent speed. We detrained at Barlin at 3 p.m. and marched parallel with the railway line in the still pouring rain to Hersin-Coupigny, roughly about an hour's jaunt. No one knows where one's regiment is; the nearest you ever get is that so and so division is in a particular area and you are dispatched with the crowd going in that direction, not necessarily to the area, only in that direction. A few miles extra marching did not matter the slightest. In these dispersal centres the divisional numbers are called out and you 'fall in' as directed. In due course the party moves off into the unknown. Other than we are wearing the same uniform; we are total strangers. It was 7 p.m. when we eventually moved off and after a couple of hours marching our little party arrived in Aix-Noulette and went our individual ways. The marching men simply faded away as all old soldiers are supposed to do. I slept the night by the ruins of the church, the rain had turned into drizzle.

Tuesday, 29th August

After managing to scrounge a couple of hard biscuits and a mug of tea I began to enquire the whereabouts of my battalion. The first hour was fruitless but slightly encouraging. They were in the line – but the line stretches from the sea to Switzerland; they were at Bouvigny-Boyeffles when I left for the Lewis gun school. If the normal routine operated, they were due to have been relieved from the 'Dugout line' the day I left and they probably have gone back up the line again. It seemed reasonably likely that I would find them thereabouts. My intuition was almost correct and after a two-hour trudge in the apparently everlasting rain, I rejoined my old pals holding the line just before mid-day.

Fritz seemed to know I, now a professional Lewis gunner, was on my way, and did his utmost to prevent my arrival by shelling the support lines with a lot of heavy stuff. When I eventually reached the firing line I was told that they had been subjected to almost continuous shell-fire ever since they had taken over and had suffered many casualties. The intensity and accuracy left no doubt in my mind a lively time was in store for us all. Returning to the line in the middle of a bombardment after a week of peace and quietness gave my nerves a severe jolt. I felt very uneasy for a little while but I was with my pals again, men of my own breed far away from the make-believe 'Camp Wallahs'.

Wednesday, 30th August

Still raining and the mud is up over our ankles. It is most difficult to move, yet move we must, and the more we do, the more clammy it becomes. At dawn our guns opened out on the Ridge. Fritz retaliated, as we knew they would, not on our gun positions in the rear but on us stuck in the mud. The poor, bloody infantry get it both ways; there is nothing we can do except stick it out and hope for the best.

Thursday, 31st August

We handed over our positions in the sunken road to the 'Drakes'. If their name is anything to go by, they should feel at home in the quagmire whilst we are high and dry in the huts in Bouvigny Woods. The following night we are back on the Ridge digging a cable trench from 7.15 p.m. to 4 a.m.; the exact whereabouts I do not know, but what I do know is that we suffered many casualties from both rifle and shell fire.

Saturday, 2nd September

Repeat performance of last night only the fire is even worse. We slog our guts out trying to get some cover, not that a shallow scratch in the chalk is of any earthly use against the heavy stuff that is bursting amongst us, but we feel much safer even when we know it is really silly.

Sunday, 3rd September

After tea, my section now reduced to six men, are detailed to guard the bomb store at the 'French dump' on the Arras-Béthune road. Quite a small dump, merely a hole in the roadside about six or seven feet deep, the sides timbered and a roof of corrugated iron covered with sandbags and loose earth. Entrance is gained by a short rough ladder leading from a hatchway in the roof; the floor is covered with duck-boards that are somewhere beneath about six inches of stagnant water. A sump-hole near the foot of the ladder enables the occupants to keep the cess pool under control. One man has to always be on duty with a canvas bucket; his constant efforts save the ship from foundering and the motley crew from drowning. With the bucket filled from the sump-hole he has to climb the ladder and empty its muddy contents without leaving the ladder. If he is a bit nippy he may reach the sump-hole before the water seeps back in again. All through the night, GS waggons bring up more and more boxes of bombs, all sorts and sizes and they have to be stored somewhere down below. Working parties from the line with chits for certain types that had arrived in boxes but leave in sandbags. If, as the result of all this man-handling, a pin works loose from one of the Mills type, that's the last we see of it, or its carrier. Some nights are reminiscent of Guy Fawkes, never a dull moment.

Wednesday, 6th September

In the early hours of the morning the bomb store was set on fire. There had been a lot of shell-fire during the night. An unexploded shell may have caused the minor conflagration but the total disregard we had for danger could not be ruled out. There was no fixed light or lantern in the store, we had to grope our way about by candle light, balanced on one of the boxes while we handled the almost continual flow of bombs in and out. The seat of the fire seemed to be in one of the recesses; dense smoke made the removal of the stored boxes very difficult and the ever increasing muffled explosions forced us to vacate the place. After about five minutes sheltering in a neaby shell-hole there was a terrific bang and bursting bombs showered the area. The waiting parties that had called to collect their quota didn't bother to collect; they simply faded away. It would have been useless anyway as Fritz seemed to increase his firing for quite some time. As the fire-work display from the store had ceased some time ago we re-entered the store but the fumes soon drove us out. This annoyed us very much as we felt much safer under the cover of a few inches of loose earth, at least, from the rain of flying splinters.

As dawn broke the shelling ceased and the mist gradually cleared, revealing the night's damage; a gaping hole at one end of the store; one recess completely obliterated, but the others more or less undisturbed. As the smoke and the fumes had dispersed, we began to make the necessary repairs and almost made the place ship-shape when our relief arrived; our spell of support duty was over. Soon after dark we relieved the 'Drakes' in 'Kellet' line. This was an awful trench. Fritz shells it continuously and there is absolutely no shelter. Our whole time is spent repairing the damage to our trench.

Thursday, 7th September

I was instructed to report to the Lewis gun section holding the 'Dugout' line. A change is as good as a rest, so they say, but the change of scenery lasted less than an hour. I was delighted that the knowledge I had acquired at the school was to be put to some use; instead of firing single rounds from my rifle, I would be able to fire a magazine of 47 in less than five seconds; only the slightest pressure on the trigger was all that was needed. The Petty Officer in charge, Tommy Edgell, enquired my name, number, next of kin, religion, size of my boots etc., before allocating me to a gun's crew, none of whom I knew. Almost before I knew what was happening I was on my way back to the firing line I had left less than an hour ago. My dreams of blasting hell out of Fritz was severely shattered. I was, like all new boys, at the bottom of the class. Number One fired the gun, Number Two fed it; and the rest of us filled the magazines that Number One could empty much quicker than we could fill them but we always had a good reserve to start with. I soon found out that all the crew were experts and a grand bunch of chaps. Number One could make the gun talk. Number Two was his equal.

Friday, 8th September
At an hour before dawn, it was the strict order of the day that all troops in the line must 'stand to arms', that means that all work ceases and everyone stood on the fire-step if possible, in readiness to ward off an attack. The powers that be seemed to believe that all attacks must come within that hour. Of course they didn't, but the opportunity was always there. Under cover of darkness the enemy could crawl forward unseen and there were always plenty of shell craters for him to wait in for his barrage to open up. The distance to be covered was considerably lessened in this way, for the element of surprise was essential. Today's dawn was heralded in by a dawn chorus, not of birds, but by men in the village of Angres that was held jointly by Fritz and us; he had the major portion of the ruins. The singing was very good; it was refreshing and continued long after the sun rose. For an hour or so, the war was forgotten, I am at peace with my mind and sanity has returned to my brain. The sun seems brighter than usual but I know its sometimes mocking ways. It can make everything look bright and clean, yet in reality it is dark and unclean in the shadows – and there are many shadows.

Saturday, 9th September
Our artillery bombarded Jerry's line all day and he sent a few over

in return. Then the trench mortars came along and sent dozens of 'Stokes' over and, as usual, cleared out leaving us in the firing line to cope with the backwash; '*Minnenwerfers*' wobbling as they came towards us and thus making their direction uncertain. Their destructive power when they finally land, is enormous, the blast alone blows one off the fire-step. The watching and waiting for them to land drives me half crazy, there is nothing I can do except stand and shiver. They scare the life out of us all even before they finally drop, scattering thousands of hot splinters that scythe through the human corn stalks already drooping from the blast.

Sunday, 10th September
At dawn Fritz seemed to think that it was his turn to show off his artillery and the tempo increased as the day dragged on. As usual, our front line was his target. His aim is perfect but the line is thinly held, more correctly, thinly manned. In our state, we couldn't hold anything, we have had nothing to eat all day. We could hear the swishing of the *Minnenwerfers* but couldn't see them. It is difficult to see anything, the noise is terrific, the destruction tragic, the reaping of the human harvest is almost complete. We who are left will have a lot of gleaning to do, gathering up the remains of the lads you have come to know so well, it is a sickening fatigue that nobody ever gets used to. Every time I place an arm or a foot into a sandbag I cannot help feeling that, but for the grace of God, it might have been my own. This everlasting slaughter is proving absolute nothing.

Monday, 11th September
Shortly after midnight a slight cool drizzle began to fall; it was refreshing. We hastily repaired our battered trench. There was much to do before daylight. On the whole, the night had been quiet – the uneasy quiet that follows a bombardment. We were able to talk quietly instead of shouting as we filled the hundreds of sandbags and placed them in position, each one adding to the cover we sorely need and each one worth its weight in gold. As the hours went by we achieved reasonable cover and were able to walk about freely in an almost new trench. Our gun position now altered, we

fired off a couple of magazines to get our line of fire and to let Fritz know we are ready for 'battle to commence'. We need not have bothered as the trench mortar crowd arrived in the line. At 4 a.m. they began their own battle with hundreds of 'Stokes' being hurled towards the enemy lines with amazing rapidity. It looks so simple; the mortar is allowed to slide down the short barrel on to the striking pin and out it comes. They appear very destructive even though they are small compared with the paint drum size of the *Minnenwerfers*. After firing their quota they hurriedly depart and I don't blame them; they know that Fritz will retaliate and they certainly did with a few extra for good measure.

Tuesday, 12th September
We were relieved from the firing line and took up a position in support only a few yards to the rear. It's known as 'Dugout line' but I don't know why. As far as my crowd are concerned there are no dugouts. However life is not so tense; the hour on, hour off does not apply in the support line. In any case, we are seldom in the actual trench during daylight hours, we are for ever carrying rations, ammunition and stores of every description from the rear and during darkness we are out in 'no man's land' as covering party to the men digging or repairing the barbed wire. The constant shelling of the last few days has severely damaged out trenches and blown wide gaps in our wire which have to be closed. It is an unpleasant task and a lonely one; cramped in a wet shell hole for hours and watching for any movement in the shell-torn wilderness, far ahead of anyone and knowing full well that the lads are relying on us to give them warning; hoping we will be able to find a gap to enable us to regain our line just before dawn. Each night the routine is much the same.

Saturday, 16th September
I have just returned from a cold all-night spell out in 'no man's land' and, as is the custom, I have cleaned and oiled the gun. My hands were so cold that I had difficulty and I was so tired that I wanted to close my eyes but I knew I must not. My Lewis gun is not only my friend, but a friend to us all. If the Jerries attack, it will

keep them at a respectful distance. As a baby needs its mother so it needs our constant care and finds attention twenty-four hours a day. Above all, it must be kept clean like other babies. Our precious monster is very tempermental at all times; it needs protection from the cold and its oiling is a work of art. The slightest amount too much is fatal as it becomes sluggish in the cold air; instead of assisting the feed-arm, it hinders it, as does the minutest particle of dust. Our baby monster, inhuman in its ways and devastating in its action, has a delicate constitution. Having completed my task sitting holding the baby on my knees, my eyes closed automatically, I could hear the Petty Officer addressing me but I didn't want to know him, or anyone else for that matter. I was exhausted and only wanted to sleep. A sharp kick on my shins brought back my senses but my eyes refused to function. I thought I heard him say: 'You're going home; you are for Blighty, my lad'. This news alarmed me. I felt my person – I must be wounded, yet I felt no pain, I must be dreaming. Another kick and I was fully awake.

'Come on, my lad, on your hind legs quickly or I won't let you go.'

'Go where?' I asked.

'To Blighty, as I said.'

'It's real then, I'm not dreaming.'

'No, it's real enough, you're not dreaming; It's just come through. Report to Company Headquarters at once. I'll take charge of the gun. Go on now, be off before I change my mind; and keep your big head down on the way out.'

Normally very talkative, I lost my tongue, I was speechless. I tried to wish him luck while I was away, the move I tried, the more incoherent I became but I did manage to shake hands before leaving. I still could not believe it as a few moments ago I was dead tired and couldn't keep my eyes open; everywhere was dark and miserable, now everything looked bright and gay. The tiredness had fled like a haunted deer before the hounds and I was full of life and joy. I was on my way home after nearly two years of fighting on three widely separated battle-fronts and a soldier's dream was coming true.

As I made my way along the trench to the Company Headquarters I shook hands with all and sundry but my elation suddenly turned to fear, I felt myself shivering; I was cold yet the sweat was pouring from me and I was unsteady on my feet, I was afraid lest something might happen at this vital moment and blow away my long felt hopes of seeing my home just once more. If the High Command decided to attack in the next few hours, then all leave would be cancelled. Jerry might have the same idea in mind if he knew I was going home. Every shell that came over – and there were many – seemed to be aimed at me. There were many quite near misses, every one more terrifying than the last. I could see in my fuddled mind a sniper loading his rifle with a bullet with my name on it as I crept into the Company Headquarters.

Under cover of a flimsy water-proof sheet I regained my self-respect and felt composed as my company commander gave me my instructions; so many that I began to feel important. The interview was friendly; he spoke like a father to his favourite son and even apologised for the lateness of my leave, but now I would soon be on my way. Reminding me that the reputation of the battalion depended upon my behaviour whilst on leave, he handed me my leave form together with Form AFW 3337, instructing me to digest it before leaving. Instructions for officers and men proceeding on leave AFW 3337.

1. Rifles will be taken but no ammunition. This will be left with unit.
2. In addition to ammunition it is strictly forbidden to take on leave any of the following: bombs, shells, shell-cases, trophies captured from the enemy, and uncensored letters.

   If any of the above articles are found to be in the possession of men, their leave will be cancelled and they will be returned to their units.

   A written report will be made by the Base Commandant through IGC.
3. Combined warrants and tickets to destination and return to be obtained from unit before departure. The station of destination, not merely the country, must be inserted on the warrant.

4. Men will be collected into parties in such formations as may be ordered at Rail-heads under Officers detailed for the duty. The senior officer will be in command of the party and be responsible that the men entrain together and are marched on board the ship and kept together whilst on board and are marched off and entrained together at port of arrival. The same procedure will be adopted for the return journey, the same officer collecting his men together at Victoria Station or Waterloo the men will be expected to assist by rejoining their proper parties as quickly as possible.
5. Pay to be obtained before leaving the unit. French money will be exchanged at Victoria Station or Waterloo. *Not* at port of Departure.
6. Any delay on the journey should be vouched for by the following who will endorse the pass:

   From Unit to Home:

(A) Delay between unit and embarkation by MLO or OC Rest Camps.

(B) Delay on the sea voyage by Embarkation Officer at port of Arrival.

From Home to Unit:

(A) Delay on railway in Great Britain by RTO at station at which that part of the journey is completed where the delay occured.

(B) Delay on sea voyage by MLO or OC Rest Camps at Port of Disembarkation.

No one else is authorised to grant extension of leave on account of delay.

7. Officers and men are reminded that it is their duty to give no information of a military nature to anyone whilst they are on leave in England. Information which is widely known in England soon reaches the enemy and the success of military operations may be endangered thereby. Non-observance of the above will lead to cancellation of any present leave granted to the offender and the stoppage of all future leave.
8. A copy of these rules will be given to each man with his leave form.

I tried to read the form but I was much too fidgety. I had waited so long for this moment and I wanted to be on my way in case the powers that be changed their minds. I had climbed out of the crater of Hell and was perched perilously on the rim, a sudden change of wind could hurl me back into the flaming mass I knew so well. After what seemed hours and hours of waiting my Company Commander instructed me to make my own way to Hersin.

'It's a fairly long tramp but you'll manage it. Good luck, Murray, now off you go.'

My journey home had begun and the trench system on the Lorette Spur was soon left behind. It was dusk before I reached Aix-Noulette and I was advised to take the left fork at the ruined church. Although I had made up my mind to press on regardless, I could not resist having a quiet sit down in the ruins as I had done on many occasions, it seemed so peaceful; the crucifix still clung to the shattered wall, yet there was evidence of more shelling since I had last seen it. It was almost dark before I took the left fork that I understood would bring me to Hersin. Arriving at yet another cross-roads at Boyeffles, I decided to sit down and wait for someone to come along so that I could be directed. I must have fallen asleep as it was dawn when I awoke, stiff and very cold but in the best of spirits. I was away from Dante's Inferno and on my way home, even if I had to walk all the way to the Channel.

Sunday, 17th September

I reached Hersin bright and early and in excellent spirits. I reported as instructed. With others on the same mission I was told to wait further instructions.

'You can get something to eat over there,' someone shouted out.

I enjoyed a good breakfast and sat on the door-step so to speak. More hours of waiting before we boarded a bus that took us to Béthune, arriving just before noon. At once we boarded a train and were soon on our way to Boulogne, arriving at the docks at 3.30 p.m. When our leave forms checked and found correct, we boarded SS *Victoria*. A pleasant journey of a little more than two hours in the brilliant sunshine. In this direction it would have still been pleasant even if the old tub had gone sideways. With no mucking about for a change, we disembarked at Folkestone where a special train was waiting to take us to Victoria station. Our reception was really wonderful; Dozens of elderly, middle-aged and young ladies insisted that we ate the buns and drank the tea offered, everyone smoking 'buckshee' cigarettes, members of the YMCA and Church Army assisted us in every possible way, no request was refused. In a matter of minutes I replaced the string in my boots with brand new laces and, while I was on the job, gave my feet their first airing for weeks. I believe I was in imminent danger of being lynched when the whistle blew for us to board the waiting train.

The war was a long way away as the crowd of helpers waved to us as the train moved very slowly away from the station; like us, it was reluctant to leave such helpful people. We were given the same treatment on arrival at Victoria; special guides to direct us to our respective stations, tea-urns and stacks of sandwiches and buns, willing men and women doing their utmost for a train-load of scruffy, lousy, happy but very tired heroes from the battle-front. I changed my ten franc note at the exchange bureau for eight shillings and made my way to the underground train that would take me to King's Cross. Even with two changes, Charing Cross and Euston, the journey did not take long. I arrived at 7.45 p.m. with exactly one hour to wait for the next train to Newcastle. As at other stations, there was plenty of people to advise the strangers to London.

There was one chap spouting his head off half-way along the platform to a croud of about thirty eager listeners, which I and several others in uniform, joined. He was a forceful speaker; the war was of Satan, it was all wrong and it was against the teachings of Christ. So far, so good, but he allowed his enthusiasm to run amock when he said those of us in uniform were disciples of the Devil. We were poor timid sheep being led to the slaughter; could be, poor; yes, very poor, even with my eight shillings. Disciples of the Devil, maybe, sheepishly led to the slaughter, could be, but timid, dear me, no! This was too much for the Jocks and the Tynesiders who were desirous of putting our worthy conscientious objector on the right track; that is if the rail track was the right one. It was certainly the easiest and had the desired effect of putting an end to his tirade, at least while we were about. I had the feeling that some of the civilian members of the crowd did not approve of our rough methods but in their wisdom kept their feelings to themselves. We were birds of passage and this platform a temporary resting place. We would soon take flight again to fresh fields and pastures new; there would be no undue dalliance and each moment was precious as we have few to spare, we are still under the temporarily suspended sentence of death.

We cheered the train as it pulled in very slowly but we cheered even louder when she pulled out at 8.45 p.m. with us on board. I now felt that I was really on my way home.

CHAPTER SIX

Leave at Last

Monday, 18th September

I alighted at the Central Station, Newcastle-on-Tyne at 3.20 a.m. and, on making enquiries I found that the first local train to Lintz Green was not until 7.58 a.m. This gave me ample time to have a wash and brush up. Not that I was concerned very much with my beauty but I did need freshening up after my long, tiring journey. Afterwards I made my way across the High Level bridge to call upon my Uncle Bill and Aunt Maggie in Gateshead whom I had not seen since Christmas-time 1914. Breakfast appeared as if by magic and I thoroughly enjoyed my first meal on leave. Gateshead was always my brother Tom's first port of call on all his furloughs; it was also his last when returning to his ship. I had followed in his footsteps, for it would also be my last port of call when the time came for me to leave for overseas. There was no need to mention it; it was routine and taken for granted and everyone was satisfied. It was home from home.

During my short stay I had figured out that if I sent off a telegram just before I caught the local train to Lintz Green, it would be delivered at home only about five minutes before I arrived. My father and brothers would be at work and I didn't want to give mother a shock by just walking in the ever open door. The train journey would take half-an-hour and then there was a two mile walk from the station. I didn't hurry, though I wanted to, lest I should arrive before my telegram. I took the footpath that ran parallel with the North Eastern Railway as far as Friarside and then continued up the colliery line as far as Rose Cottage where a bridge carried the road, the only road, that led to the station. Long before I reached the bridge I saw someone waving, it was my mother. My telegram had arrived ten minutes earlier; the local postman had made a special journey on his cycle before going on his round. The postmistress had told him Mrs Murray would be very pleased and he guessed the rest. Mother had left at once just as she was, no coat or shawl and in her carpet slippers. She was still panting for breath, afraid to go any further in case I came by the road, utterly exhausted she collapsed when she let go of the railings. Our greeting was made sitting on the wet grass. I carried her the rest of the way home.

The kitchen was full of steam from the iron kettle she had placed on the roaring fire. I had reached home and that was all that mattered.

After the inevitable cup of tea I asked Mother to get out my civilian clothes. She said there was no hurry but I knew there was. I was lousy and told her so. I undressed in the back yard and jumped into the rainwater butt; she brought me soap and towels and a jar of Condy's crystals, the only carbolic available, but very effective as I found out later. The itch was far worse than the lice. I was quite used to their affection. However, I felt fresh and clean and that was the object of the exercise. My more or less public bath amused the neighbours but though I couldn't have cared less, they were very discreet; a friendly wave and a shout of 'Welcome home, lad' really meant something. I was able to scramble out of the butt, but not without some minor difficulties even though I had lost most of my modesty on the far-off beaches of Gallipoli. I was not the first conquering hero to have returned to the village; but many never returned. Those of us that did felt we were cheating. The casualty list from Gallipoli after 4th June had shaken them but the current slaughter on the Somme had stunned the village; almost every home had received the terse, fateful telegram, quite a few homes had received more than one. The youth of the countryside had gone, never to return and many more would join them; it was only a question of time. I had survived much longer than most of my school-boy friends and was very pleased to be home again for a few days but the thought of my meeting the bereaved, distressed me very much. The idea of the local employer forming his own battalion from his workmen; the mine owners and the 'big-wigs' glorification in establishing the 'Pals' or the 'Chums' battalions propaganda-wise was very patriotic. It took maybe twenty months to organise, recruit, train and dispatch overseas and less than twenty minutes on the Somme to annihilate them.

My 'civvies' were neatly folded on a cracket near the rain-butt as though they had only just arrived from the cleaners but, try as I may I could not get myself dry enough to dress, I gave up and came indoors. The very wet towel around my waist marked my route towards the roaring fire in the kitchen-cum-dining room. Progress was easy now until it came to the buttoning-up. My shirt was at least an inch short in the neckband but it covered that part of my anatomy that mattered. The trousers had shrunk or my posterior had enlarged as I could not hold my tummy in long enough to even get one button fastened and had to give up the struggle, my elder brother's Sunday suit fitted perfectly round my waist but the legs were ridiculously short though I was able to sit down in comfort and of course more tea was brewed and had to be drank.

Mother was busy in the front room at the sewing machine. A huge gusset was sewn in the back of my trousers in a matter of minutes, my shirt was changed for an open-neck type I had worn in my cricketing days. Soon I was fully dressed and respectable providing I wore a pull-over or kept my jacket on to hide the gusset. To avoid being offered more tea I went visiting the next-door neighbour. The men folk were at work but Mrs Ellis was such a friendly soul. I had left her comforting Mother when I left for the wars in 1914 and she would do the same thing this time when my short leave came to an end. I felt I must thank her as I might not get another chance. Apparently she was expecting me as I walked through the open door. The doors in the mining villages of the north are always open; one never knocks as there is no need; one just walks right in and makes oneself at home. If the family are eating you will be offered what there is going and no one is offended if you refuse. Someone may be having a bath in front of the fire; the wife might be washing her husband's back; it's all in a day's work.

Mrs Ellis had made a fresh pot of tea specially for me and between us we drank the lot. I began to wonder if the gusset would stand up to all this tea drinking. Returning to my own back yard, I noticed smoke coming from an old outhouse and promptly opened the door to investigate, I wished I hadn't as the dense sulphur fumes almost choked me before I managed to get the door closed again. Mother had declared war on my unwelcome guests firmly established in the seams of my trousers. For the next hour I suffered much more than I had done during a real gas attack. Mother was certainly making sure that her fumigation would be successful and I had no doubts at all as it nearly killed me. It was quite sometime before I was able to breathe freely.

I decided to take a walk and inhale some of the wonderful fresh air blowing over the surrounding hills. I had no particular port of call; just a free and easy stroll. I had plenty of time as my father and brothers would not return from work before 4.30 p.m. at the earliest. Up hill and down dale I ambled alone with my thoughts at peace with the world. I remember reading somewhere that man is much less alone when he is alone. My goodness this is true; my mind is overflowing; meetings and conversations of years ago were as clear as crystal, I could discern my companion who had been with me when I carved my initials on this big beech tree; the bark has done its best to overgrow the scars I had made but as yet, had failed to obliterate them. A little lower down on the other side, I knew exactly where to look, were the initials of my schoolmate Walker Anderson, but he will not revisit this beech tree, at least, not in body, for he lies in a foreign field that is forever England. I must call on his folks; he would have wished me to do so. There are so many who will never return. What shall I say? What can I say that will not in some way distress them? My very presence must bring sad memories, yet I must go. They were my schoolmates so I must call upon the other two who will shake my hand and hear my voice but will not see me for they are blind, and there are those who have lost an arm or a leg or both, and four doors away I must call on Armitage, my rival on the cricket pitch. He has his sight and all his limbs but was so riddled with machine bullets whilst advancing alongside me on 4th June his limbs are now useless. I dread the days that lie ahead so much that I will not record any more of my leave. I doubt if I could even if I tried. It *is* possible to be sad and happy at the same time. I arrived back home just after noon to find

rmitage Jewitt who lived three doors from
e, and was severely wounded on 4th June 1915.

'Lucky Durham' (my nickname) on leave in September 1916.

my father and brothers already washed and dressed. Word had reached them in the mine that I had arrived home. They had packed up at once and came home. No more work whilst I was on leave.

Tuesday, 26th September

Today is my last day on leave and I shall have to leave home about 9 p.m. to enable me to catch the last local train at Lintz Green at 9.32 p.m. Time moves at an alarming pace when one is on leave. I have had some distressing moments but I have enjoyed the change, the conversations and; above all, the friendliness of the villagers. Dear old Mrs Reilly has given me a bottle of Irish whiskey to give to her son, a sergeant in the Northumberland Fusiliers.

'He is in France; you can look him up, it will be nice for you and him to have a drink together. I know he will be pleased to see his old workmate as he often spoke of you before he was called up as a reservist.'

The odds of my meeting him must be about three million to one but it would have been cruel to shatter the dear old lady's dream; I've seen so many dreams shattered. I promised I would do my best and left her the happiest woman in the village. Perhaps the only one that was happy. I finished my round of calls and after tea asked for my uniform. The Flanders mud and the blood stains had gone; my 'grey-back' shirt was almost white and the tunic and trousers were neatly pressed. My string mending had been replaced by a neat patch that made it unnoticeable from the outside. I was so neat and tidy that one would have thought I was on my way to Buckingham Palace instead of the mud of the Somme. I felt clean but I knew that within twenty-four hours I would be standing up to my knees in the claggy slime of a trench and the home comforts would only be a far-off dream.

This is by far the most distressing part of any leave; the time to say good-bye. Even more distressing when one is leaving to face the firing squad. This is no fantasy, it's a statement of fact. Everyone that lives to relate his feelings, if he is truthful, will freely admit he knew all the time that he had very little hope of survival and this would be the final good-bye but the most important thing was not to show what was uppermost in his mind but must make-believe and show the flag. The general feeling of the lads in the line was that, upon rejoining the regiment their chances of living more than a few days were very slender. It happened so often. I know of many cases: one chap was blown to pieces as he was re-entering the firing line, another of my pals lasted less than one hour and many survived only a few days. It seemed fatal to go on leave, a sort of a final concession by the powers that be, and yet I know of no one refusing to accept the challenge. With those ugly thoughts in my mind, my final handshakes were much firmer than my hopes of ever returning but, once out of doors, with my mother being consoled by Mrs Ellis as usual, I felt normal as I ever hoped to be again. The local train to Newcastle, a quick visit to Gateshead, the inevitable cup of tea and another parcel of sandwiches for the journey, I was almost full pack with eatables and a bottle of the hard stuff that does you good at any time, when I boarded the midnight train to King's Cross. As at Christmas-time 1914 there were more servicemen on the running board than inside the carriages when we pulled out of the station. Upon arrival in London shortly after 6 a.m. there were plenty of people to direct us to Victoria. These guides certainly knew their stuff; they seemed as anxious to get us on our way to Dante's Inferno as they were to get us on our way homewards. I have no quarrel with them; they do a grand job.

Time was not so pressing today and I had ample time to make certain that I reported on time at Victoria station. I made my way there and having dumped my luggage, set out to explore the Westminster area. I had long since learned that a good soldier never lets go of his rifle, not even when he sleeps (that is, when he gets a chance to sleep) as it is his best friend, at the moment, my only friend in this vast city. I'm not the only lonely individual though everyone appears to be alone, everyone going somewhere and in a hurry to get to their destination; strangers in a city of strangers.

With my best friend slung over my shoulder and my pace the regulation 27 inches, I was soon mingled with the motley crowd, in strange surrounds among a host of strangers, but not for long. I had company – two big sturdy Red Caps with the crease in their trousers so sharp and defined that I kept my distance for fear of being lacerated. They demanded in no uncertain manner, to see my pass. Having satisfied their curiosity I had the freedom of London for the next hundred yards until more Red Caps, more enquiries, more suspicion. I thought I would have a rest from them in a tea-shop but I was mistaken. I was accosted everywhere I went and in the end I walked down the Strand, not with my gloves in my hand as Burlington Bertie did, but with my leave pass ready for inspection. It didn't make much difference but it saved a little of my precious time. I suppose the order to leave all ammunition behind in France before proceeding on leave was a well thought-out instruction to avoid the total elimination of the Military Police in and around Victoria station. Many of the fighting men were not as sober as the regimental sergeant-major would wish, but there was nothing he, nor the battalions of Red Caps could do, that would be worse than our immediate fate. Accidents could, and do happen even in the best of regiments. We were under no delusion about our chances of living. We were all under the sentence of death, the question being, 'How long have we to wait?' The firing squad were waiting with their rifles already poised, waiting for the kill. All our calculations were on an hourly basis and these blasted Red Caps were cheating us out of these hours. Because of their constant interference, we fighting men hated them more than we did the Germans. After all, the Germans we come in contact with are, like ourselves, fighting-men but these so-and-so's are dodging the column. Much more of their arrogance and I'm afraid I shall forget about the reputation of the battalion. I know they have a job to do as there are a lot of drifters floating around but anyone with only half an eye could pick out men that have experienced continual bombardment for weeks on end. We are drunk with fear; it is written on our faces and our minds are befuddled. We are not human any more; we prowl around in the manner of haunted animals always aware of the lurking danger yet ready to fight for that little bit of life that is still within us.

Although I had over an hour before I was due to report I entered Victoria Station and mixed freely and easily with the 'pukka' soldiers. My home leave had ended and under military discipline, I, as a soldier again, should soon be off to the wars. I was among soldiers who know what war is. I felt very relaxed, maybe because I had said my goodbyes before leaving the North Country. Quite a lot of these lads have still to say theirs. It's a heartbreaking business, the mothers, wives and sweethearts, the old dad and the younger brothers and sisters; they were all here; some struggled to keep back the tears but most failed miserably and were miserable indeed. Old dad appeared to have fortified himself for the occasion and tried his hand at telling a tale but his joke fell flat and only by sheer determination he prevented himself from falling as flat as his joke. But he meant well; they all meant well. Total strangers shook us by the hand and wished us 'Good Luck' and a safe return soon. I could feel the warmth and sincerity of their good wishes. It was all very friendly but I was not sorry when we were ordered to board the train to Hell.

Upon arrival at Folkestone the SS *Victoria* was waiting alongside for us and, as soon as we were aboard she cast off for her two and a half hour's crossing to Boulogne. The weather was fine and warm, the sea calm, both coastlines were visible for almost the whole of the uneventful crossing. As soon as we were alongside we disembarked with the usual indecent haste and were marched to Choppin's rest camp. The leave trains, and the other trains as well I suppose, were run under a code letter in an attempt to keep the movements of the troops secret. There must have been thousands of us paraded in front of various large letters. A burly, red-faced, spick-and-span sergeant-major mounted a platform and bawled out in the fashion always adopted by sergeant-majors. I know that the incessant bombardments may have impaired our hearing but this fellow's roar would awaken the dead, perhaps it is for that reason that he has never been anywhere near the firing line.

'I will call out your divisions and train letter, you will "fall in" at the double behind your divisional letter.'

After what seemed an eternity, the thousands had melted away and only two lonely men, Chief Petty Officer Tobin and myself, remained on the wrong side of the letters, two lost souls that apparently belonged to nobody, orphans of the storm, nobody's children, in full gaze of the thousands of accredited brethren. Only two with nothing to do and nowhere to go, outcasts it would seem. In due time the sergeant-major vacated his platform and with his abundant staff retinue, appeared before us, more red-faced than ever, out of breath, stunned and, for some time, speechless. Nothing like this had ever happened before; well, not since the guardsman dropped his rifle at the Trooping of the Colour in the long forgotten days of peace-time soldiering. An apparent mutiny on his pet parade-ground. Words failed him as he stood glaring at the two mutineers who had refused to 'jump to it' on his word of command. Yet we did not appear defiant and there was no outward appearance of any insurrection or even insubordination, just two unloved and unwanted, lonely seraphims, standing so unconcerned while the war waited and a small army looked on helpless. The uncanny silence was broken as the sergeant-major had regained his breath. His face muscles ceased twitching and I could plainly see his chest expanding; now for it.

'Why didn't you fall in behind your train letter when I called out your division?'

Chief Petty Officer Tobin: 'No, sir, you have not called out our division.'

'Who are you then?'

'One Chief Petty Officer, One Ordinary Rating, 'Hood' battalion, Royal Naval Division, Right of the line and pride of the British Army.' Then a belated 'Sir'. (Tobin's naval rank made him senior to the sergeant-major.) Apparently the sergeant-major had called out the 63rd division. This was the number given to our division but unknown to us until much later. However as Tobin had insisted we were naval personnel, the whole atmosphere changed. No more bawling or shouting, no right turn, quick march. We ambled away in our own good time and found our own train letter. The Navy, all two of us, received the respect, and rightly so, due to the Senior Service and the division retained the respect of all throughout the war. No one sniffed at the Royal Naval Division, including the German High Command. History had been made not only on the battle-fields but also on the parade ground at Choppin's rest camp.

The parade was dismissed with the instruction to reassemble at 6 p.m. We were free to go and do as we pleased until that time. Most of us spent the rest of the afternoon sampling the wine in the town and dodging the Red Caps and the brass-hats, almost a full-time job. Because of this dodging, we drank more wine than we would have done, or should have done, with the result that the parade at 6 p.m. was farcical. Most of the lads were unable to stand and many didn't bother to try, but at 6 p.m. we managed to help each other to stagger to our respective trains and promptly fell asleep. Our train left Boulogne just after midnight.

CHAPTER SEVEN

Entrenched on the Front

Thursday, 28th September

I detrained at Béthune in the very early hours of the morning and stretched out on the platform until eight o'clock. I have not seen Tobin since boarding the train at Boulogne; he is my company CPO and we should be both going the same way. Some of us were ordered to board a bus actually on the move, where it was going nobody on it had the faintest idea and I really don't think that the sergeant, who ordered us on it, knew himself. The general policy seemed to be, get everybody moving out of sight and things will sort themselves out somehow.

'Get on that bus that is just leaving or that one standing over there. Perfect strategy – out of sight, out of mind. Wherever you are dumped the procedure is always much the same. If there are not any buses available you are ordered to chase after a column that has already moved out and after a mile or two your column catches up with the column in front who are apparently trying to catch some other wandering crowd. Strange as it may seem, everybody eventually finds their own mob.

About noon our bus arrived at Ourton, its terminal. The rain that had been falling since last night turned to a cold drizzle. The sun was doing its best to break through and the four-hour journey had not been too bad considering the shocking state of the roads. No danger of falling off to sleep on such a journey; much more likely to fall off the bus altogether. The prospect of a little march was very welcome but the question was, in which direction? No one knew; the battalion was somewhere in the area but exactly where appeared to be a mystery or a very close secret.

After many enquiries I was able to deduce that the 189th Brigade were allocated to the villages of Fresnicourt, Monchy Breton, Hermin, Magnicourt and Frevillers. I was advised to make my way to Houdain which meant I had to go back the way I had come by bus for about three kilometres, then turn right at the cross-roads and another three or four kilometres would see me in Houdain. Upon arrival there I was advised to follow the main road for yet another four kilometres roughly and then take a side road on the right that would, if I chose the correct side-road, bring me to Hermin where I might find the 'Hood' battalion resting. It was almost dark when I eventually arrived, very weary and worn out, to be told that the battalion were out doing field training. 7 a.m. to 7 p.m. That is apparently the Army's idea of resting, but we have got used to it by now. It was nice to be with the lads again. I was so pleased to see them as they were to see me, even more so when I opened dear old Mrs Reilly's whiskey. I had resisted the temptation long enough. How we enjoyed drinking the sergeant's health; for some reason he had enlisted many years ago in the name of Thompson and as Sergeant Thompson he was later awarded the highest Russian decoration for bravery in the field.

Friday, 29th September

Still very dull but dry when we set out for further 'battle practice' which lasted all day. To my mind, we have had enough battle practice but one must not be allowed to get stale. There is not much chasing in the forward trenches so we make believe we have Jerry on the run all the time we are out of them. If and when the time comes to chase him in reality, few of us will have much chase left in us, anyway the signs of a breakthrough in the near future are not very imminent.

Saturday, 30th September

We set out for a divisional route march in the pouring rain. Wet through, we marched kilometre after kilometre, hour after hour, with a ten minute 'fall out' by the roadside at the end of each hour. These route marches are normally lengthy affairs and this one was no exception.

Late in the afternoon we marched past our Brigade GOC, Brigadier-General L.F. Phillips. These more or less ceremonial parades are significant to us as they are the only time we ever see our General, but we know that when he takes time off from pondering over his maps to inspect his troops, it means that our destiny has already been sealed. We are the little flags that his staff, miles behind the firing line and comfortably seated, will move forward as the attack is in progress; the reports will be many hours out of date by the time they reach headquarters. 'The so-and-so battalion, attacking on the right flank, have captured their objectives and are firmly established after much stubborn resistance by the enmy.' Of course, by the time the report reaches headquarters, the so-and-so battalion may have been thrown out of the enemy's line and recaptured it several times, with a few survivors clinging on by the skin of their teeth to what is left of a trench and waiting for another inevitable counter-attack. The dead are silent and the pitiful cries of the wounded lying out in the open, slowly bleeding to death, are not heard way back at headquarters. The little flags will be moved forward and those moving them will be very pleased. Thank goodness someone will be happy. I know of many that will be sad indeed, way back home as well as out here.

After eighteen months of almost continuous fighting, all the glamour – that is, if there ever was any – has gone out of war. All that remains now is the hope of survival. If a particular division is good at trench digging, wiring or carrying, then it seems to get all the jobs of that nature when the men ought to be resting. If it is, in addition, good at fighting, then it is thrown into the attack until decimated, reinforcements will uphold the name and the fame that the division has won and they too will suffer in consequence, the only question that remains unanswered is: 'How long can the human body and mind endure this torture.'

These grandiose parades may impress the General and boost his ego. He will say how delighted he is to command such a fine body of men; he will say how smart we look; how efficient we have been in the past and how well he knows that we shall uphold the glorious traditions of the division. He will take the salute as we march past on our way to the mud and the rain of lead and, having said all those nice things about us, he will return to his comfortable abode in the opposite direction, dine and wine in a manner befitting to his exalted rank; the correct brandy-glass cupped in the palm of his steady hand to bring out the bouquet, lingered over and appreciated, the Havana cigar left smouldering in the ashtray. He will then sign our death warrants and we shall perform the exequies out of sight and out of mind.

Tuesday, 3rd October

Since handing over the line to the 37th Division in mid-September, we have been in the IVth Army Corps training area and today we have spent quite a long spell at the firing range. The rain came down in torrents as usual. Each time I have visited any range, the rain clouds seem to wait for me to take up my firing position, they hover overhead causing the visibility to be reduced to nil. I fired my quota; hundreds of nickel-plated bullets into the partial darkness in the matter of a few minutes, and had no trouble at all with my Lewis gun. Where they all went I have not the faintest idea and nobody seemed to care anyway. We were all more concerned as to what part of the line we were going after all this extensive training. There was absolutely no doubt in our minds that we were to attack somewhere soon. There were a lot of strange faces in the battalion; officers, NCOs and men many of whom I had not seen since we landed in France. They had been away on some sort of special instruction and are now with us, ramming down our throats the correct way to do this or that as per rule-book, all sorts of new-fangled ideas. Men who were considered in the old days as misfits were now specialists in their own particular branch of warfare. Of course, this did not apply to all of them but it did to many. However specialized they were it was too late in the day to try to teach grandmother to suck eggs.

Our short sojourn in these pleasant Artois villages was nearing its end and the return of these omniscient specialists, together with previously wounded and sick, plus a new draft of reinforcements, has brought the division almost up to full strength numerically. A division at full strength is really a self-contained miniature army comprising about forty different units. Of these there are only twelve first-line infantry battalions each with its own Lewis-gun section. Batteries of artillery attached on loan more or less, light, medium and heavy trench-mortars, companies of Field Engineers, heavy machine-gun section, signals, field ambulances, divisional train with their horse-drawn General Service waggons, ammunition column, ordnance, sanitary, mobile veterinary section and a Pioneer battalion, in our case the 14th Worcestershire Regiment, who served us extremely well at all times.

Our division up to now had never fought as a complete unit. We have always been on loan to other divisions in bits and pieces. On Gallipoli we were attached to the glorious 29th. They actually taught us volunteers how to fight and how to stay alive. They were excellent teachers, so much so that the pupils became almost, but not quite, as good as their masters. Some of the 1st Brigade and the 3rd Royal Marine, Brigade, were with the Anzacs at Gaba Tepe. 'Anson' battalion took part in the landing at Suvla Bay. At Cape Helles the 'Hood', 'Howe' and 'Anson' battalions of the 2nd Naval Brigade were loaned to the French and fought under the French General d'Amade during the general attacks of 6th, 7th, 8th and 9th May. For a while during May, some Anzacs were attached to us under Sir Archibald Paris, KCB.

From now on, we were to operate as a complete unit under our own General. The various incidental units function as pillars and corbels and are most essential, but the keystone of the arch are the twelve first-line infantry battalions.

There is a very strong rumour that we are to try to recapture some ground on Vimy Ridge, lost sometime before the Somme battle began. We have spent some time in that area and it was on the Ridge that we had our baptism of fire on the Western Front.

Wednesday, 4th October

At three o'clock in the morning, we left Hermin in the pouring rain and, after three hours' marching, arrived at the village of Ligny St Flochell, near St Pol, and eventually boarded the train at ten o'clock. Even so some time elapsed before we got moving. All the early afternoon we spent in a siding – waiting for darkness, some said. It was eight o'clock in the evening when we detrained at the rail-head at Acheux and marched to Forceville with the rain still pouring down. The barns were of the usual type – plenty of fresh air, for the village had had more than its share of enemy shelling. The whole area had been devastated long ago but by now it was quite peaceful; at least for the moment it appeared so. It was almost midnight before we managed to get settled down. The rain had ceased but the night was perishing cold and our wet uniforms did not make us more comfortable.

Thursday, 5th October

Apart from the local working parties, we enjoyed an easy day. We had a new interest; we had heard of a new weapon, the Tank, but apart from a glimpse of them at the rail-head at Acheux, we were in the dark as much as everyone else as to the precise nature of this wonderful new weapon that would make our job as infantrymen a piece of cake. These monsters would flatten the maze of barbed wire, they would overrun the machine-gun posts and trenches alike. All we had to do now was to follow in their wake and mop up. They could, and would, demolish everything in their path and rifle-fire was useless against their armour-plating. They could span any known trench, climb down and out of any crater. They would win the war on their own. Here they were, about a dozen of them, huge clumsy brutes, squatting on the hard unshelled ground, stationary and silent. My first thought about them was to wonder if they were capable of any movement as they looked so clumsy and so heavy. They had reached this far by rail but the rest of the way would be over shell-torn terrain. We, light-weight youngsters, sink up to our knees in the slime; these heavy-weight monsters would sink out of sight without trace. I had been taught, and know from experience, that speed was an essential factor in crossing 'No man's land'. That being so, the thousands of shells that have fallen on this area every day for months and the constant rain has turned it into a quagmire.

On Salisbury Plain these iron-clad tortoises no doubt can do all those things accredited to them, but out here at this time of the year when everywhere is water-logged, they don't have a remote chance of showing their real value. If however they can flatten the huge heaps of barbed wire, made even more entangled by the constant shelling they will save the lives of many infantrymen as these heaps cause the attacking men to cluster in the gaps to be 'sitting ducks' for the opposing machine-gunners. At this moment we are prepared to believe in anything that might end the present stalemate of trench warfare.

Friday, 6th October

The rain has ceased at last; the first really fine day for quite some time but it is very cold during the day and even colder when darkness fell as we wallowed our way through the mud, in many cases knee keep, where a shell had scored a direct hit on the communication trench, and the resultant crater was filled with stagnant, evil-smelling water. The firing line was worse for the constant rain had caused the sides to collapse and it was no longer a trench – it was a wide, muddy ditch. The men holding the line had to be dragged out of the freezing mud, only to get stuck fast somewhere else when they in turn attempted to haul us out. All night long we were extricating each other and no other work was possible. The picks and shovels we had brought with us were absolutely useless and had been lost somewhere in the slime. The shovels could not contain it; it was labour in vain. The more we tried to bail out the more the sides slithered into the unholy quagmire but the exercise kept our circulation going. We were able to move more easily through the claggy mess by using our shovels as paddles to assist us, for move we must. The Very lights were hovering overhead, revealing the sea of mud out in front, the bisecting shell craters filled to over flooding with stinking water, reflecting the eerie lights as they drifted slowly earthwards. One normally stands still while these lights float slowly over 'No man's land' under penalty of death from a bullet from the ever-watching, fantastically accurate sniper. Tonight it's Hobson's choice. The poor devils on our right in the valley must be far worse off than we are on the slope.

Monday, 16th October

For the last ten days we have been working up the line and in front of it, trying to make the trenches more habitable. We Lewis

A once peaceful woodland in the valley of the Ancre.

Traffic jam on the Somme. The effect of a single shell can well be imagined.

gunners take up positions ahead of the working party, in shell holes often waist-deep in water. Nights in these conditions are very long nights indeed. At dawn today, when the working party had returned to the front-line trench, we crawled back almost frozen stiff to begin the long trudge to our barns in Forceville. On our arrival we were told that Major-General Sir Archibald Paris, GOC Royal Naval Division, had been severely wounded and Major Sketchley, GSO2, had been killed near the village of Mailly-Mailly whilst on a visit to the 190th Brigade holding the left flank of our divisional sector. Some say it was on the 12th and others the 14th, but the actual date does not matter. The loss of our General does. Everyone spoke well of him; he had been in command of the division since 1914 and was the last bulwark between us and the Army. We were Naval personnel and fought under orders from the Admiralty whilst he commanded. Now he has gone; what will happen to us?

At sundown on a fine evening, we left our roofless barns at Forceville and had hours of wearily slithering in the mud, constantly tripping up with rifles entangled in the endless signal wires that seem to be stretched at every angle. These journeys to and from the line are exhausting affairs. Today's trudge takes us to the Knightsbridge sector, a little to the right and deeper in the Ancre valley; deeper in the mud. It's the same old routine; for ten days we have expended much energy making a particular part of the line reasonably habitable under very trying conditions; now we have taken over another quagmire and we shall have to start all over again making things ship-shape if we are to survive.

Wednesday, 18th October

Much to our surprise, we were relieved by the 'Howe' battalion. They came up with the tide and brought the rain with them. The ecstasy of being relieved after only two days was, however, short-lived. At the back of our minds we knew it was too good to be true. Instead of taking up a position in the support line, we took over the firing line, yet a little further to the right with our right flank on the bank of the overflowing river Ancre, immediately in front of the village of Hamel. My company's right flank was the road that winds its way along the flooded valley towards Beaucourt, a little more than a mile to the north-east. Good God, what an awful place! Will the rain never cease? It is impossible to even try to do any reconstruction and there is certainly much hard work to be done, everywhere is flooded. Jerry out in front must be much better off as he is holding the higher ground, the Beaumont-Hamel, Beaucourt-sur-Ancre Ridge. He has held the ridge for years and has resisted all attempts to dislodge him, and there have been many since the Somme offensive opened on 1st July. On that day the 29th Division suffered enormous losses; the Newfoundlanders, in particular, were annihilated. Jerry holds all the aces while we wallow about in the mud, fed up and far from home. A few hot meals would help to thaw us out but this is wishful thinking; an occasional swig of rum would be appreciated but it's ages since we had our last tot. Some people manage it, we don't.

Thursday, 19th October

After a very cold and miserable night we continued with our hopeless task of trying to make the place ship-shape. The constant rain has caused the sides of the trench to fall away; it is now barely three feet deep, that is, three feet above the water and sludge level. The two feet of sludge is quite a problem and we just cannot make any headway. As fast as we throw out the slime it runs back in; in fact we have actually made the ditch wider and considerably more open in an attempt to get some cover from the constant shelling. Out of sight, out of danger, they say; at the moment we are neither. A worm can wriggle away when danger threatens but we have to stay knee-deep in semi-frozen sludge, hoping for something to happen. All conversation ceased long ago, we are numbed to the core, human marionettes.

Some of the ration party that left hours ago have returned and are greeted with a half-hearted cheer as usual. Something is happening and dinner is about to be served. The bully-beef stew, like the coffee-coloured tea, is stone cold. Come to think of it, the stew in colour and texture is not unlike the slime we are wallowing in. All of us have lost our likes and dislikes long ago and no orderly officer is likely to come around to ask if there are any complaints.

He has the same menu, maybe a little warmer than ours, that's all. Many moons ago I made up my mind to eat everything that was put before me and be sharp about it, though I must confess that at times it has been most difficult to stick to my vow. Today, it's as usual, Hobson's choice. The ration party have done their very best; they have plodded their way to and from the support line and an Army dixie of stew is an awkward thing to carry at the best of times and they are not to blame for the lousy weather, nor the unchanging menu.

Apart from the shelling there is little to report; it goes on and on without any signs of a lull. Only maniacs would attempt to attack in these conditions but, as we are all completely mad, we have to keep a sharp look-out all the same, just in case Jerry has a brainstorm. With the going down of the sun (though we have not seen much of it lately we know it's up there somewhere) it has become much colder. Our slime has considerably solidified and we are able to make some progress in clearing our ditch. We can move about much more easily. We have scraped a lot of the mud from our puttees and have settled down for the night, a watchful night as always, with one hour on look-out and one hour off to sleep and dream of the comforts we left behind years ago.

Friday, 20th October

Shortly after dawn the rain ceased with the rising of the sun but it is still perishing cold. Daylight and sunshine seems to give us a new outlook, a new vision that clouds out the miseries of an uncomfortable night, a new day is born and we are somewhat surprised at being alive and able to move about. Yesterday is a thousand years ago and today there is work to be done. We have got off with a promising start. The tea was quite warm at breakfast-time but the bread was frozen hard like the mud that encases us from head to foot. The tea has recharged our batteries and we set about our task of rebuilding our trench, interrupted yesterday by the constant shelling. With the exception of those on look-out duty, all available hands were engaged filling sandbags and building the trench wall interrupted only by an occasional shell burst. We all feel much better and safer now we have something to shelter behind. On the whole, the day has been quieter than of late. A few men have been sent down suffering from cold and exhaustion but no one in our vicinity has been injured by enemy action which is quite comforting.

Late in the afternoon we were relieved by the 'Hawke' battalion and commenced our long and arduous trek to the rear, eventually arriving at Englebelmer utterly dead to the world. Whilst awaiting allocation to our respective barns, a nine-inch shell, by the sound of it, burst amongst us, killing, so it is estimated, twenty-eight and wounding many more. It is ironic that having survived those horrible days and nights so close to the enemy, one sees one's pals blown to pieces so far away from the firing line, but in war nothing is real, nothing is explainable, things happen and that's all there is to it.

Saturday, 21st October

Most of the day was spent trying to get cleaned up but as we expected, it was a hopeless task. One blessing was that it was fine but very cold and so dull that I thought my watch had stopped, a common occurrence in this sort of weather. Even when out of the line there are continuous fatigues, we never suffer from boredom for the want of something to do. I have just returned from a dump in this vast wasteland. It's useless trying to put a name to this or any other place in this neighbourhood; they all look alike. The name 'dump' is appropriate – mounds that were once habitations, whether villages, large or small, or isolated but cosy farmhouses, or maybe the home of a local character famed for his eccentricities. All that way of life has long since gone and in its place are huge heaps of broken bricks and cesspools, the result of thousands of shell bursts. Having added to the pile of picks and shovels I made my way to my barn and flopped down on my private heap of straw, thankful for the rest. But it was not to be, for within the hour we were on our way to the firing line and beyond. The Engineers had placed a line of white tape where we were to dig an assembly trench. We call these shallow trenches in 'No man's land' jumping-off trenches. For obvious reasons they are only dug at the last moment prior to an attack. They lessen the distance the first wave of the attacking infantry has to cover before reaching the enemy's firing line. Of course, at the first sign of daylight, or even before actual dawn, the enemy patrols may have made their report. If so, the enemy will know that an attack is imminent; only the exact time is not known.

The advanced trenches are doubtless of advantage to the attacking force but they are a hazard before the actual attack and must be occupied by a skeleton force to prevent the enemy from entering them. While the actual digging is in progress, patrols are positioned some fifty yards or so away, in shell holes nearer to the enemy's trenches. They are usually Lewis gun crews. Immediately before dawn the digging parties retire to the front line and then to the back areas; some of the patrols are left to garrison the partly dug assembly trenches during the oncoming daylight hours.

During the Gallipoli campaign the trenches were so close (in some cases only ten yards separated the opposing forces) that the method of an advanced starting trench was out of the question. The strategy being almost the opposite to that employed on the Western Front. In 1915 artillery was very scarce, and machine-guns (we didn't have the light Lewis Gun in those early days) dominated the battle. The firing line was occupied by the maximum of troops available and the support line, some twenty yards or so to the rear, was likewise garrisoned and so were the other trenches we had captured on our way forward. The whole defensive position was not more than a couple of hundred yards deep. Here on the Western Front, the enormous increase in artillery has altered the strategy and such is the concentration of guns of various calibre, that the whole defensive position can be wiped out in the matter of minutes, leaving the road clear for a general breakthrough.

On Gallipoli we could not afford to lose an inch of ground, let alone a whole defensive system. Out here in France the position is entirely different. In order to save casualties, the foremost trench is held by a few outposts, watch-dogs as it were. The second trench, known to us as the support line, is perhaps some two-hundred yards behind and is garrisoned by sufficient troops to counter-attack in the event of the enemy gaining a lodgement in our front line. The third line, a quarter of a mile or even more behind the support lines, is always fully manned.

On paper this system is wonderful but, in my experience, we are never capable of supplying a ration party, let alone a defensive bulwark in case of a surprise attack. We are scattered all over the place, doing all sorts of fatigue duties. We are absolutely useless as a defence force but the fatigues have to be done and we, the fighting men, not only have to bear the brunt of battle but have to do the humping to and fro as well.

Sunday, 22nd October

It was nearly mid-day when we arrived back in Englebelmer, utterly exhausted after a fourteen hour stint. The cooks had expected us long ago apparently as the bacon (no eggs, thank you) was shrivelled to a cinder. The tea, though, was well boiled. The condemned men ate a hearty breakfast at noon. There were no orders, no instructions, so we made ourselves scarce and were soon stretched out on the straw-covered floor of what is left of our barn. The heat of our bodies soon converted the frozen straw into a slimy mess but we were much too tired to do anything about it except to watch the miniature, misty haze hovering overhead – an *ignis fatuus*. My eyes closed automatically and my mind wandered in its own particular way. Days, weeks and even years flitted backwards and forwards without rhyme or reason, everything was so clear; long forgotten episodes appearing as though on the silver screen in a cinema.

The arrival of a salvo of heavy stuff close by brought my dream to an abrupt end. Lathe and cow-dung plaster flew in all directions and our barn, only a sorry looking skeleton of its former glory to begin with, was on the verge of total collapse at any moment. The little privacy and shelter we had from the freezing blast a moment or so ago was now gone. The ancient timbers that had withstood the rains and the wintry blasts for many years and had given shelter to cattle and many weary, footsore soldiers was now only a heap of firewood.

In the fading light immediately after tea, we were on our way again to 'No man's land' into the jaws of death, like the Light Brigade in Tennyson's poem but at a much slower pace. We trudged through the quagmire at a snail's pace until the shelling ahead of us brought the column to a halt. After a short while we retraced our steps; no one told you to but, like a lot of sheep we just followed the chap in front. He turned round so we did likewise. Where we were or where we were supposed to go, none of us had the remotest idea other than we were trying to reach the firing line. Time marched on but we stood still, almost embedded in the slime of a communication trench. After a while we, like Dick Whittington, turned again though not towards London, but towards the inferno immediately in front of us. There was not so much shelling now and our progress was reasonable considering the amount of telephone wire that seemed bent on wrapping itself around our feet as well as our rifles.

Eventually we reached the foremost line and entered 'No man's land'. We passed over three very shallow trenches roughly twenty yards apart and the lads began to dig another one, having been reminded that they were late and must get a move on. They were conscious of the fact that they were to lead the attack as soon as the weather permitted and set about the job like demons as we would have to occupy these trenches on the eve of the attack. Happily, the night was fairly quiet and everyone seemed satisfied with the night's work considering our late arrival. Our return journey was accomplished much quicker than our forward trudge.

Monday, 23rd October

Another all-night stint out in 'No man's land'. We were hoping to have a night off but it was not to be. The incessant rain had delayed the preparations that have to be made before an attack and these assembly trenches were an essential part, for we had to be concentrated as near to the enemy trenches as was possible without his knowing, before our barrage opened on his front line. The success of the operation depended upon the attacking infantry keeping in touch with the creeping barrage as it moved forward. In the 'black areas' there is intensive activity, day and night, wherever you go; men in sections, platoons and even in companies are moving about, going somewhere. There are guns of all shapes and sizes, with their limbers, and horses steaming in the frosted air add to the already heavy mist and scatter the poor, unfortunate foot-sloggers wearily plodding along, uncertain of their whereabouts, their destination, or even their fate, but giving full throat to the soldiers' song 'Mademoiselle from Armentiers'.

My own crowd were scattered about by the road-side when the order to 'fall in' in battle-order was given, much to everyone's surprise as some were on fatigues; some were trying to make some shelter amongst the ruins of the nearby barns in preparation for the coming night. Quite a number of us had not heard the order but were soon made aware of it and within half-an-hour we were on our way towards Mesnil, a small village in the valley of the Ancre. Battle-order means exactly what the name implies; water-bottles must be full, iron rations are issued, (cast-iron hard biscuits supplied usually by Huntley and Palmer), haversack, normally carried on the right side but now carried on the back taking the place of a much larger pack. The meaning is obvious; we are fully equipped for battle.

There are no houses or barns left standing now in Mesnil as they have been blasted away long ago. Only cellars remain but they are very comfortable providing one does not suffer from claustrophobia as there is only one entrance and very little light. Even so, they are a great improvement on the barns so far as shelter and comfort is concerned. I'll settle for cellars every time.

Wednesday, 25th October

I feel like a new man; we all do. No fatigues other than the local ones. I spent most of my time rummaging among the ruins and found lots of things I did not like. Several of the bodies had a finger missing which means that not all the ghouls are in the enemy ranks; we have them also.

Prior to the opening of the battle of the Somme on 1st July men were concentrated hereabouts as we are now. On this side of the river Ancre the initial attack was repulsed with terrible losses. According to my platoon officer, Sub-Lieutenant Hart, no less than five major attacks since, met with the same fate and there is abundant evidence of this round about. Be that as it may, here we are, ready for another bash.

Thursday, 26th October

Very heavy showers soon after dawn and the icy cold wind has put an end to my 'sight-seeing'; the whole place is dead. On the ground nobody is moving but in the sky there is considerable activity. Several planes appeared from the dark clouds and were almost immediately out of sight. Again and again, the sound of machine-gun fire is heard. It is amazing how these frail machines withstand the twisting and turning; the general manoeuvre seems to be to get on the other fellow's tail. The counter-moves are fascinating; a very steep climb, almost perpendicular, or an instant dive. Two of them fell in the manner of huge leaves. I think, and hope, both of them were German. They disappeared beyond the high ground just inside the enemy lines. The fight continued, but the ever-threatening clouds obscured my view though the dog-fight was not finished. A short while later one of our machines emerged from nowhere at full throttle and exploded in our main street; the only street. I and others, approached the bonfire, through curiosity, I suppose. But there was nothing we, or anyone else could do; the pilot must have been beyond all help long before the funeral pyre.

Friday, 27th October

Heavy showers and low cloud as usual greeted the dawn but they were not our main discomfort. The enemy saturated the village with all sorts and sizes of shells, lots of them gas shells. High explosive and shrapnel we can discern but the gas shells are a different kettle of fish. When they land they do not make that ominous crunch. Their arrival is almost silent; they make the sound of a dud. There is no mistaking when the other stuff arrives and it is quite common practice for some of them to be duds. We are accustomed to the putrid smell of the high explosives, so when gas shells are mixed in during a bombardment we tend to ignore all smells and thereby hangs the danger. There is always a fusty smell in deep cellars and our nostrils are accustomed to inhaling polluted air; after all, it's the best available. Our cellar is not very large but it's a happy place. Our little bunch have been together for quite a while and most of us fought side by side, more or less, on Gallipoli. We are at the moment, under the direction of our song-leader. Leading Seaman Jacky Charlton, giving full throat to a parody on that lovely Irish song, 'Where the mountains of Mourne roll down to the sea'.

The old Gal-li-po-li is a terrible place,
Where the boys in the trenches the Turks had to face,
But they never murmured, and smiled through it all;
Very soon they expected Achi Baba to fall.
At least when I asked them, that's what they told me
And in Constantinople we would have a fine spree.
But if the war lasted till doomsday
It's there we would be, where the old Gal-li-po-li sweeps down to the sea.

The morning we landed I'll never forget,
As we stood on the beach with our clothes wringing wet,
Although we were soaking right through to the skin
We didn't have time to dig ourselves in.
As we rushed over the brow we came under fire
And lots of our chums got caught on the wire,
But those that were free, went forward doggedly
Where the old Gal-li-po-li sweeps down to the sea.

We took several trenches before we could stop,
For we had old Johnny Turk right on the hop.
When he saw the caps and the tallies we wore
He just turned round and fled without asking for more.
He cried 'Allah, Allah', but that was no use,
For we were determined to take no excuse,
So we gave him the bayonet which meant RIP
Where the old Gal-li-po-li sweeps down to the sea.

We don't grow potatoes or barley or wheat,
So we're aye on the look-out for something to eat.
We're fed up with dry biscuits, greasy bully and ham,
And we're sick of the sight of that apricot jam.
We like steak and onions, fried ham and eggs
Or a nice big fat chicken with five or six legs
And a drop of the stuff that begins with a B,
Where the old Gal-li-po-li sweeps down to the sea.

While up in the trenches wild rumours we hear
It's enough to make any man go on the beer,
They say that we are all going home very soon
But I'd sooner believe there's a man on the moon.
They say that in Blighty they are waiting for us
And when we arrive there will be such a fuss;
But we didn't believe them for we would still be
Where the old Gal-li-po-li sweeps down to the sea.

Several of our motley crowd are more at-home in the mining villages of South Wales and, like all Welshmen, they have lovely voices. Their rendering of that old patriotic army song, 'Comrades in Arms' is always a joy to listen to. Unconsciously we straighten our backs and puff out our chests; we are no longer troglodytes, we are marching men. 'Beneath one banner floating along, To honour or to death gallant comrades in arms, To win the fight, with all our might ...'.

The curtain fell, not the one on the concert hall stage, but the sackcloth makeshift over the entrance to our cave. The applause brought tears to our eyes before we had time to find our gas-masks. Jacky ordered all hands outside and was the last to leave in true naval tradition. The bombardment continued as we sought shelter from the flying shrapnel and debris. All around men were coughing and spitting as they groped about with closed eyes in an attempt to ease the excruciating sting. Stretcher-bearers, ignoring the shell-bursts, tended those who could not help themselves. Some of the severely wounded were carried away, but by no means all. The bombardment continued; the oncoming shells have no eyes, they

Pat Kelly and Sid Buckley were both killed on 4th June 1915 at Gallipoli

do not see the Red Cross armbands. Time and time again, the stretcher-bearers and their wounded are blown sky-high, but others still carried on, fulfilling their mission of mercy regardless of the cost. We, who incidentally could be their next mud-covered patients, have great admiration for these brave and devoted chaps.

At nightfall the rain ceased and, thankfully, so did the shelling. We cleared up the mess and settled down, hoping for a quiet night. Fortunately, none of our section had been seriously affected though all of us had to pay a visit to the first-aid post.

CHAPTER EIGHT

Preparing for the Attack

Monday, 30th October

Our stay in Mesnil has not been at all comfortable; almost continuous rain and a good deal of shelling. Since the middle of October, we have been in the front line and the reserve trenches, always ready to stage an attack at two days' notice. Every time the date was fixed it had to be postponed for a day or so on account of the rain having made the terrain impossible. Today we were told that the attack had been postponed indefinitely. Normally we would have taken over the firing line as we have had our period in the support.

In the late afternoon we moved further back in the pouring rain to the village of Hedauville. On arrival our section was allocated a barn which actually had a more or less complete roof. Strange to say, it had stopped raining as we settled in. No shelling by either side and no fatigues. What a lovely change. Even the snoring did not prevent us all from having a very comfortable night's rest, the first for a considerable time.

For the last month or so we have been almost daily reminded that if we are to hold on to our gains further south, we must make considerable progress during our coming attack astride the river Ancre. The Beaumont-Hamel/Beaucourt-sur-Ancre ridge must be captured at all costs. The initial attack on 1st July was repulsed with very severe casualties. The huge mine underneath the Hawthorn ridge had been detonated ten minutes before the time arranged for the advance and the resultant crater had been promptly occupied by the enemy; furthermore, gaps had been cut in our wire several days beforehand to enable our men to go forward but the German barbed-wire was still intact. Our old pals during the Gallipoli campaign, the immortal 29th Division and their gallant comrades from Newfoundland, were easy targets for the enemy machine-guns whilst negotiating these gaps and very few survived to reach the enemy wire. Several subsequent attacks met with the same fate. We were left in no doubt of the gigantic task that lay before us at any moment, weather permitting.

Wednesday, 1st November

For as long as I am spared to live, this will always be a day of sad memories. Two years ago my brother Tom and all his ship-mates were lost when HMS *Good Hope* was sunk whilst in action by a squadron of the Imperial German Navy, off Coronel in the Southern Pacific.

Fate was especially kind to me today. We were on the move again but this time, away from the fighting zone. After a little more than four hours' marching we arrived at Puchevillers and soon settled in for the night. A hot meal of bully-beef stew was served as soon as we arrived and, since this would be our final meal of the day, we soon had a bonfire of straw in what was once a farmyard. For some little time we were unmolested and were enjoying a Turkish bath, fully clothed; the steam coming from our wet uniforms. It had simply poured down throughout the four-hour march and this steam bath was most comforting. Other small groups had the same idea but all good things come to an end. The stentorian voice of the Chief Petty Officer to 'Put that fire out' seemed to re-echo from every nook and corner, reminiscent of the days on Gallipoli when it was understandable as we were never out of the range of rifle-fire. Out here in Puchevillers, we were miles from the fighting area.

Thursday, 2nd November

As usual, it was raining quite heavily when we paraded in readiness to go back to the line but after standing for three hours in the freezing rain, the order to go back was cancelled and we returned to our barns, wetter than ever.

Friday, 3rd November

It was still raining; we paraded on some open ground nearby and, again as usual, we stood around for hours eventually to be told that we were to be inspected by the GOC (63rd) Royal Naval Division, Major-General C.D. Shute. Now we know why we are a comfortable distance from the danger area.

During his address to his troops, I was standing immediately in front of him and could almost touch him. He began with the usual blah, blah – how well we look, how good soldiers we were and so on; we have heard it all before. It would have been more appreciated if he had said how sorry he was that we must be very wet and cold, but maybe he was short-sighted. However, he didn't pull any punches when he got going.

'Very soon you will be called upon to wrest from the enemy one of his strongest points on the Western Front; many previous attempts have failed but I have every confidence in you. I must warn you, however, that the more prisoners you take, the less food you will get as they must be fed from your rations.'

A direct instruction straight from the horse's mouth; now we know just where we stood. After the inspection, we, the 'Hood' battalion were presented with our cap badges, but not by the General. Now we are somebody's children and we have cap-badges to prove it. Hitherto we have felt somewhat naked without some sort of label, but now we are fully dressed.

Saturday, 4th November

The first fine day for over a week. We began our return to the forward zone. The four hour march saw us back in Englebelmer again by the late evening. What remains of this little village seems to have some magnetic influence over all and sundry. There is no end to the continual stream of every conceivable form of warfare passing through; artillery pieces of all shapes and sizes, horse-drawn eighteen-pounders bouncing like shuttlecocks as they negotiate the huge potholes; the big fellows towed at a snail's pace; marching infantrymen, scattered every few yards by the fast moving eighteen-pounders, or dawdling behind the monsters. The enemy, occupying the higher ground a mile or so away, cannot help observing this massive concentration of men and artillery; they can probably hear it.

Sunday, 5th November

Our hopes and fears of a break in the weather were brutally shattered as we plodged through the mud to the front line in the pouring rain. We collected either a pick or a shovel from a dump in the support line and continued forward for a further hundred yards or so to what had been a respectable trench until the dawn retaliatory bombardment before we could attempt to re-dig the trench. Normally we Lewis gunners had enough to carry; apart from the actual gun we had umpteen panniers of magazines and additional ammunition. As there was no trench left we could not take up a position. The gun team's Numbers One and Two were left behind in the support line to look after our gun and gear while we went forward to tackle the mass of tangled barbed wire that impeded any progress in any direction, a most exhausting and painful task. As the hours passed, these bad-tempered heaps were dragged somewhere near where we thought the parapet of our trench should be and the job of re-making the trench began in earnest. At best, all we could do was to make a passage through the slime that would afford some measure of cover during the daylight hours, knowing full well that all our efforts would be blasted out of all recognition by tomorrow's dawn bombardment. We knew also, that as soon as this blasted rain ceased for a day or so, the powers that be would order us to attack and capture that higher ground, the ridge immediately in front of us, extending from Beaumont-Hamel to Beaucourt-sur-Ancre.

At the opening of the Somme battle on 1st July the Germans held this important high ground and have resisted all attempts to dislodge them. At the outset in July, the element of surprise was in our favour; the weather was perfect, the ground was hard and dry; the whole front had been blasted, night and day, for a whole week and the majority of the attacking force were fresh troops. Yet at the end of the day, those who had survived the holocaust were back in their original trenches.

Monday, 6th November

Late in the afternoon in the teeming rain we vacated Englebelmer and took over the firing line known to us as the Hamel sector, deep in the Ancre valley. In several places there was no sign of a trench, only shell-holes filled with mud and slime which caused us to scramble about in the open. Each crater, many of them quite deep, overlapped the next, and as we tried to move along the rims we often slid into the watery slime. It was no easy matter getting out of the quagmire only to slide into adjacent morass. However, knowing full well that just before dawn our artillery would open up and Fritz would retaliate at once, we managed to make some sort of cover which could not be called a trench but would have that purpose. The only thing in our favour was that the sodden state of the whole area would allow the high-explosives to bury themselves deep before exploding and we would be bespattered with clods of soggy clay instead of being riddled with red-hot shell fragments.

Tuesday, 7th November

This atrocious weather is getting the better of our nerves. We seldom have any conversation with each other. Movement is difficult and in any case there is nowhere to go. In some strange way Fritz relieves the monotony when his artillery opens up with a really deafening roar. The rain-drops are reinforced with shrapnel bullets against which we have no shelter at all; we feel so helpless as we await our fate. After a while he increases his range and most of his shells go beyond us and land in the villages of Hamel and Mesnil. We, in turn, take full advantage of the lull and set about repairing the damage to our ditch. We patch up the wounded but that is all we can do for them; they will have to wait until things quieten down considerably. Some will have to remain for a much longer period; their fighting days for King and Country are over. Even so, they will not be allowed to rest in peace. Alive or dead, there is no peace here. Maybe some day we will all come to our senses but these days will never be forgotten however long we survivors may live.

Friday, 10th November

Our period in the forward trenches during the last four days has been extremely exhausting; almost continual freezing rain and subjected to more than usual shelling. Our sector of the line swings backward until it reaches the railway line running parallel to the river which is in full flood and overflowing the normally marshy bed of the valley. The dawn chorus is not from the birds, for they have long since deserted us and I don't blame them, but from the deluge of screaming shells that appear to be just above our heads, creating a wall of fire about two-hundred yards ahead of us. It is by far the most concentrated bombardment so far and has continued for much longer than usual. Maybe our newly positioned guns are registering as some of the shells are falling very short. We expect to be shelled by Fritz but take a very poor view of being blasted by our own people. Somewhere up amongst us there is an observation post occupied by an artillery officer and a signalman whose job is to correct the range, but you cannot correct anything until it is found to be incorrect and by that time the damage has been done. In the meantime the PBI have to grin and bear it. What annoys me most is that I have never met an artilleryman who will admit that some of their shells do fall short. But apart from all that, they do a grand job and we are most grateful and always will be for without their help, I and many others, would have been kicking up the daisies long ago.

Sometime before midnight we were relieved by the 'Hawke' battalion and, after much puffing and blowing, arrived back in Mesnil to be allocated not the cellars but shelters cut into the railway embankment, miserable cubby-holes with sheets of corrugated iron covered with about six-inches of loose earth forming the roof. Inside there are two tiers of wooden bunks with rusted wire-netting for the occupants to rest their weary limbs and on the floor duck-boards floating in about a foot of stagnant water. Those fortunate chaps who manage to occupy the upper bunks are in clover but those less fortunate ones, like myself, down below have to cope with the continual dripping from their clothes and the snoring chaps above, but in spite of all this, a good night's sleep was enjoyed by all. In our exhausted state no sleeping pills were required. Just to cheer us up we were told that we were 'standing by' in readiness to move off at a half-hour's notice. There is no doubt in our minds as to the direction the move will be. In the meantime there are only the local fatigues to do. We are waiting for the referee to blow his whistle to start the game as the weather improves even just a little, for time is getting short.

Sunday, 12th November

After an early breakfast sitting among the ruins we were issued out with all sorts of paraphernalia. Each man has a couple of ordinary bombs to carry in his pocket and some were given a special 'P' bomb. These are quite new playthings, not unlike longish tins of jam but containing phosphorus and are to be thrown down the entrances of the enemy dug-outs which are known to exist. After all, the enemy has occupied the trenches in front of us for years. Dinner was served at noon, steaming hot bully-beef stew and a frozen chunk of bread that needed a bayonet attack to disintegrate.

During this sumptuous meal, our platoon officer, Sub-Lieutenant Hart, told us that we would be moving out shortly as we had to be out of Mesnil to make room for the reserve troops that would be supporting us as we went forward. The weather was fine but very cold as we assembled by platoons and only an occasional shell fell among the ruins. In reality it was quite a pleasant afternoon until some bright quartermaster decided to get rid of his 'buckshee' rations. My section was issued with a tin of jam each and, believe it or not, a glass jar of piccalilli each and two sacks of bombs between us.

At exactly two pip-emma the grossly overloaded human pack-mules with their rifles and bayonet, haversacks crammed full with their worldly goods; water bottles, personal billy-cans, enamel mug dangling from their waists together with their entrenching tools beating a retreat on their posteriors and their pockets full of bombs and a sand-bag full of them over their shoulder, the Onward Christian Soldiers entered the communication trench on their way to fight the foe, that is, those that were able to stagger forward. Negotiating this communication trench was most arduous; it was very narrow, muddy and in many cases partially flooded. There were telephone wires everywhere and even an arm pushed forward in an endeavour to avoid entanglement did not have much success; we were constantly wrapped up with the confounded stuff or tripped up causing the bag of bombs to be half-buried in the slime at our feet. A wet sack on one's shoulder is bad enough but a cold muddy one rasping the back of one's neck is almost unbearable yet has to be endured.

The progress was very slow. Even so, it was broad daylight when we halted just beyond the ruins of Hamel. We were told that we would have to wait here for some time until it became dark enough for us to go further ahead. We made ourselves as comfortable as circumstances allowed in various battered trenches. During this well earned respite my pals and I decided that we had carried the jam and piccalilli quite far enough and that as none of us had even seen piccalilli before, we thought that it was not only wasteful but discourteous to throw the comfounded stuff away, so we ate the lot, with disastrous results later on. Whether the jam did not mix with the piccalilli or the other way round I do not know; I only know the results, we all did.

When it was quite dark we moved forward over the open ground following a white tape to our firing line and then, without any aid, a considerable distance into 'No man's land' before reaching our assembly trenches and thereby in alignment with our left flank. My battalion, the 'Hood', formed up in four distinct waves, roughly a man every two yards. Behind were the other two battalions, the 'Drake' and the '1st HAC' assembled in the same formation. On that reckoning, on our particular patch of 'No man's land' there were twelve lines of men lying in the open. We, who were to lead the attack, were roughly 200-250 yards from the enemy. My company, 'C' with 'B' company on our right, was in position at seven o'clock. It had taken us five hours to reach our assembly point and we had to wait another ten and three-quarters before attacking at zero hour, fixed for 5.45. We were instructed to get as much sleep as possible. There were patrols out in front to warn us of any movement by the enemy. Without any shadow of doubt, all of us could have done with a good night's rest but the prevailing conditions prevented any such luxury. In spite of all that has happened to us on Gallipoli and out here, we are still human, a little crazy at times perhaps and not worried much about what is right and what is wrong but we are still trying to do the job we set out to do when we volunteered long ago. We were once boys but not any more; we are now much older and wiser and much worn, yet anxious to finish the job. Owing to the atrocious weather we have been hanging about for so long that we are inclined to be a bit on edge but in a few hours we shall move forward and once the attack begins, no one can stop it except the enemy.

The creeping barrage was originally timed to move forward a hundred yards in five minutes but now, owing to the sodden state of the ground, slowed down to seven minutes. It is essential that we keep close behind the wall of fire and be in the enemy trench before he has time to get out of his dug-outs and position his machine-guns to simply slaughter the advancing troops as he did on 1st July. On that terrible day, the attacking troops were ordered to walk slowly so that they would not be exhausted when they reached his front line, and consequently they were mown down long before they got anywhere near his front line. We have been fully briefed about the impending operation. It is most uncommon for us infantrymen to be told anything – we must be under new management. For several days the strategy has been drilled into us.

The attack will be on an eight-mile front astride the river Ancre, four miles on either side. The Royal Naval Division's sector will be 1,200 yards immediately north of the river. The extreme left flank of the division in touch with the 51st Division leading the attack, the 1st Royal Marines on the extreme left. On their right, the 'Howe' battalion, then the 'Hawke' and 'Hood' battalions with the 'Hood's' right flank on the railway and the river swamp. The first objective of these leading battalions would be the three trenches of the German front line system known to us as the 'Dotted Green Line'. They would rest there and reorganise. The following four battalions the 2nd Royal Marines, 'Anson' 'Nelson' and 'Drake' would go through to capture the second objective, a valley through which ran a road known to us as Station Road, and beyond a trench that ran along the further side of the valley on the ridge running from Beaumont-Hamel to Beaucourt-sur-Ancre Station, known to be heavily fortified. We called it the 'Green Line'. They in turn would rest there and reorganise. The creeping barrage would concentrate on this area for some time and then when it moved forward the first four battalions, having sorted themselves out, would press on forward to capture a trench near the top of the hill immediately in front of Beaucourt-sur-Ancre – the yellow line to us. The fourth and final objective was the 'Red Line', a position just beyond the village, to be taken by the four battalions that had rested on the 'Green Line'.

The time taken to reach all our objectives would be a little more than four hours if all went well, so we had plenty of details to memorise. The creeping wall of fire would be our guide and also our timetable. Everything depended on our keeping close to the barrage. To lose it would be fatal.

In my own little mind I feel extremely proud at having been trusted with even the smallest details of the operation. I know as much as the officers, I have been upgraded (without pay); all that was missing was the General's baton. I also knew that during the last hour or so, quite a lot of us have been wandering about in 'No man's land' very close to the enemy. If by any chance any of our men have lost their way in the darkness and unfortunately finished up in the enemy's line, the thousands of men lying out in the open, without any cover at all, would have precious little time to live if Fritz opened up with his artillery and months of preparation would be wasted.

So far, everything seems to be going according to plan. The hours linger on; maybe they are going too fast for some of us. Who knows? Who cares? My bed for tonight is a shallow groove less than two feet deep connecting two shell craters; both waterlogged; and I have a sack of bombs for my pillow. Looking at the desolation around me with bewilderment, I enjoy each breath of polluted air. I liken the stagnant water in the shell hole to the ornamental goldfish pond near my home. Each shell-burst causes the stinking water to quiver and the fragrance is not to my liking. I want to sneeze but dare not. There are so many things I want to do; I want to eradicate the hardships of yesterday, the slaughter and the sorrow I must endure during the imminent holocaust. I am certain that my thoughts are shared by most of us lying out here with nothing to do but hope and pray.

It is extremely dark, I cannot see the hands of my watch but I can feel the dampness of the mist on my face and assume it is about midnight. I may be hopelessly in error but it doesn't really matter, for nothing matters any more. Each and every hour is the same. I fancy I can see a figure approaching on my left; maybe it's a ghost; I can not hear any footsteps and there is no reason for anyone to be wandering about; we are all supposed to be sleeping. After what seems to be an eternity, I realise it is no ghost; it is my colonel, Colonel Freyberg, who is having a quiet chat with the chap in the next hole to me. I sit up with much difficulty. He apparently recognised an 'old hand' maybe because I had been the Prime Minister's son, Sub-Lieutenant Asquith's, runner while we were in England, on the *Grantully Castle* during our voyage east and when we landed on the Gallipoli peninsula. As such, I had on many, many occasions the honour of addressing him with the usual preface, 'With Mr Asquith's compliments, Sir' and deliver the message.

'You, too, are still with us. So pleased to see you. Make yourself as comfortable as you can and good luck. Do try to get some sleep.'

With these parting words he disappears into the darkness.

CHAPTER NINE

Attack at the Ancre

Monday, 13th November

Just after five o'clock the whole line seemed to come alive; in my vicinity, most of us were stretching our legs. It had been a long night but, thank goodness, a quiet one. Had the enemy known that thousands of men had been lying in the open so close to him without any shelter whatever and had opened up with his heavy or even his light artillery, the casualties would have been enormous and the confusion so unavoidable, no attack would have been possible. Even now, we were not out of the wood, as there was yet another half-hour before the kick off and, in spite of all attempts to preserve the absolute silence, we were not entirely successful.

At 5.40 a.m. we fixed bayonets and remained standing at the 'ready', head and shoulders leaning forward, rifles and bayonet in front of our bodies at the 'port' position. A few minutes ago there had been some activity a little ahead of us; some bombs were thrown but as they were to the right of us, we were not unduly concerned with what was happening in the distance. In such moments as this we are only concerned in what is going on under our noses. In any case there was nothing we could do.

Our platoon officer Sub-Lieutenant Hart, gazing at his watch, had called out: 'One minute to go, men', and punctually at 5.45 a.m. all hell was let loose.

Behind us the sky reddened, which reminded me of home when the nearby blast furnaces at Consett Iron Works were being drawn. Seconds later we heard and really felt the shells of our eighteen-pounders, almost wheel to wheel, passing overhead to create a wall of fire, 150 yards ahead of us. We moved forward as quickly as we could over the shell-torn terrain and managed to get quite close to our barrage, much too close for my liking, before it began its crawl forward. Shells were falling amongst us and behind; some from the enemy and, some of our own falling short. The mist was too heavy to see what was really happening and the smoke and fumes from the shell-bursts compelled me to close my eyelids in an attempt to ease the smarting, but to no avail until the flood of tears gave me some relief.

A completely strange fragrance invaded my nostrils; it was sweeter than usual and yet it made me cough and spit. The noise was deafening. Sub-Lieutenant Hart, a couple of shell craters ahead of me, was waving his arms about frantically urging us on as we approached the first of the three trenches we were to capture. It was battered almost beyond recognition; the artillery chaps had certainly done their job thoroughly. I could see no signs of the enemy, but I didn't expect to see any as this first trench was probably a sort of outpost line only occupied during the hours of darkness by groups of two or three men whose job was to send up flares and maybe a few bursts of machine-gun fire when anything out of the ordinary was happening in 'No man's land'. They would then, if lucky, nip back to their second line which was a different kettle of fish, a line of resistance.

There didn't appear to be many of our chaps either as we pressed forward and entered his second line. Like the first, it had been bashed about but was still recognizable as a trench. A few yards to the right of my entry I came across an entrance to a deep dug-out and, without the slightest compunction, heaved one of my phosphorus bombs into the darkness. Almost at once, a cloud of poisonous fumes slowly hovered in the adit and just to make sure no one would be able to come out to molest our supporting troops after we had gone forward, I threw a couple of my Mills bombs down for good measure. There was quite a lot of activity hereabouts as the huge heaps of entangled barbed wire had caused us to bunch. In time we had spread ourselves out and made for the third line, the main defensive line, and the completion of the first stage of the attack.

The plan was that we, the 'Hood', would rest and reorganize

here, while the 'Drake' battalion following on our heels would pass through us and capture the second objective, the 'Green Line'. Unfortunately, the 'Hawke' battalion on our left had been held up by the devastating machine-gun fire from a redoubt midway between the enemy's first and second lines which appeared to have been completely missed by our barrage, and in turn their supporting battalion, the 'Nelson', went blindly on to the same fate. Both battalions suffered exceptionally heavy casualties. Only a few of the two battalions, those that were in touch with the 'Howe' on their flank, were able to pass the redoubt. It was 1st July all over again, and 'V' beach at Gallipoli also – the leading troops held up with the supporting troops suffering the same fate. There was no way of stopping them. The creeping barrage kept to its prearranged timetable whilst the unmolested machine-gunners wiped out the attackers.

In less than half-an-hour both battalions ceased to exist, leaving the left flank of the 'Hood' in the air. By virtue of the nature of the fighting, the 'Drakes' also became involved, and consequently only a handful of them, less than sixty is my guess, reached us in the 'Green Line'. With less than five minutes to go before the barrage lifted to the 'Green Line', Colonel Freyberg decided to lead his 'Hoods' and the remnants of the 'Drakes' to the next objectives, the trench in front of the sunken Station Road and the 'Green Line' trench on the ridge beyond it instead of trying to reorganize.

At the appointed time, the barrage moved forward. We followed close behind and soon overran another severely battered trench. Up to now we had been climbing uphill, but a short while after reaching this trench, we found ourselves in the sunken road that ran from the Station towards Beaumont-Hamel. After a stiff climb up the opposite side, the 'Green Line' trench was in our hands. There were many entrances to the very deep dugouts in the Station Road but our bombs had the desired effect. In fact at this moment there seemed to be more prisoners than attackers. The noise of the battle made communication difficult with them, but the point of the bayonet is understood by all fighting men whatever his race or colour.

Way over on our left a full-scale battle was being fought. It appeared to us that the strong point between the enemy's first and second lines that had caused so many casualties to the 'Hawke', 'Nelson' and 'Drake' battalions was still holding out. According to the original plan of battle, this position should have been captured by the 'Hawkes' while we were reorganizing on the 'Green Line' but it would have been fatal if the handful of 'Drakes' who had survived the slaughter in front of that redoubt had attempted to attack alone. The result of this change of plan was that the 'Hoods' were in position for the third phase of the assault a little over an hour too soon.

Punctually at 7.30 a.m. the barrage moved on for the attack on the 'Yellow Line' that ran across our front immediately in front of Beaucourt-sur-Ancre. The fourth and final objective was the 'Red Line', a position beyond the village. Having progressed quite some distance up the hill, I found myself on what appeared to be a road running parallel with the railway. Shortly afterwards we were halted because the barrage seemed to be stationary. I think we were quite close to our objective, the 'Yellow Line' as both the enemy and our own artillery were concentrating on a position just ahead of us. There were quite a lot of shell-bursts around us; whether they were the enemy's or ours, I do not know; probably both.

Whilst waiting here for the next move I was wounded by a shell splinter in the abdomen which knocked the wind out of my sails and ended my account of the battle. The next recollection I had was that I was lying on a stretcher in the village of Hamel with someone washing the mud off my face. I must have been blown up as well. After my wound was dressed I was offered some refreshment but I didn't feel so good. Later I was taken to the 3rd Field Ambulance at Martinsart. The dressing was changed and I was taken to the Casualty Clearing Station at Acheux.

After a couple of hours there I was put aboard a train to the 29th Casualty Clearing Station at Gesaincourt arriving about midnight. Quite a long time was spent here during which my wound was again dressed. Sometime during the night we were put aboard a hospital-train and eventually arrived at the 2nd General Hospital in the Casino, Le Havre. Throughout the whole journey from Hamil I was in a very dazed condition, I could not keep my eyes open but the details of the journey were given to me in hospital by another wounded chap who had been my companion all the way.

Wednesday, 22nd November

I was transferred to No 4 Convalescent Depot somewhere in the town. Men were allowed out of the depot on pass, from 4.30 till 8.30 p.m., but as I was still on dressing I could not leave the depot. This did not worry me as I had much difficulty in keeping my balance and kept falling down without the slightest warning. The food here was excellent; much better even than at home. Pay-day was every fortnight. Five francs (3s. 9d.). My sojourn here was like a donkey's gallop; short and sweet.

Friday, 24th November

We left the Convalescent Depot at 6 p.m. and marched to the station. We boarded the train immediately but did not pull out until the following morning at six o'clock, arriving at Rouen after a five-hour journey and proceeded to a camp where quite a nice dinner was served on trestle tables in the open air. The weather was fine but not very warm but the bully-beef stew, potatoes and greens were piping hot. Moreover we had as much as we wanted.

I had a morbid feeling that the calves were being fattened up for the impending slaughter, but for the moment we were enjoying every second of our freedom. The war was a long way away. In contrast to us war-worn and weary birds of passage, the strong and vociferous permanent residents of this Rest Camp were strutting about in their neatly pressed uniforms, buttons shining like little suns; we all felt out of place and that we made the camp look dirty. Amongst ourselves there was no waiting to be introduced formally before speaking; we were comrades in arms, fighting men who knew what war was all about and the value of sincerity.

Our heterogeneous mob of about fifty, having finished our sumptuous feast, were still seated at our tables awaiting further instructions when, from out of the blue came a six-foot tall sergeant, moustache neatly waxed, swagger cane at the regulation angle under his left arm, bawled out in such a stentorophonic manner that our tin mugs rattled: 'Attention'. Of course, true to form, we obeyed smartly as we always do on hearing such a command. Most of the long forms toppled over but we remained rigid until the arrival of the seargent-major: 'At ease men', was his opening remark.

We were all set to murmur his King's Regulations with him; we had heard them so often but surprise, surprise, instead of delivering a monotonous lecture in a defiant posture, he walked amongst us speaking with a quiet, cultured voice, which was almost inaudible at times. In fact I was beginning to think that my hearing had been affected. Things didn't seem real any more, especially when he said, with conviction no doubt:

'You men have had a pretty rough time of it lately. You deserve a break. Whilst you are under my orders, you are excused all duties. I want you all to enjoy to the full this short respite, and, I say again, a well-earned respite.'

He lined us up in fours. 'Right turn, by the left, quick march', destination unknown until the party was outside the camp gates when he called out: 'Halt! Pay attention, men. Your train is timed to leave at 3 p.m. My job is to see you are all aboard. I am relying on you. Dismiss!'

In the absence of any NCO I, at the ripe old age of just turned twenty, assumed command; after the Lord Mayor's Show came the dust cart. Even with much active service on three different fronts, Egypt, Gallipoli, and here on the Somme behind me I knew that 'coming the old soldier trick' just wouldn't work, someone had to take charge and do a bit of shouting:

'Pay attention, men. None of us had an earthly chance of passing through the gates had not the sergeant-major, at a considerable risk to himself, marched us out. He has trusted us and we must not let him down. All agreed? Yes. Then we shall all line up here at 2.30 sharp and enter as we left, in formation.'

We ambled away with no particular object in view, we were free to do as we please, for a short while anyway. There appeared to be an instinctive desire to keep together; we are all of the same breed. On finding ourselves outside an *estaminet* it didn't need any suggestions as to what was the proper course to take; we all entered and sat down. Those that had francs ordered what drinks they wanted, mostly *bière*; the word sounds the same, more or less, in English. Quite a number were without funds but those that had soon saw to it and no one was without a tonic of some sort, more often than not, spiced with cognac, maybe not Courvoisier or Napoleon, but nevertheless, good brandy.

This seemed to improve their vocal capabilities during the inevitable sing-song. The British Tommies' version of 'Mademoiselle from Armentiers' is not suitable for the vicar's tea-party but life out here was no tea-party. All good things come to an end, especially for fighting men whose life span is not guaranteed to reach the proverbial three score and ten. A merry, garrulous bunch did their best to assemble outside; those few that had full control of their legs helped those that hadn't. Arm in arm we ambled our way towards the Rest Camp intent on entering as we had left. It took some time to get the squad into platoon formation, but with much coaxing I eventually managed.

'Squad, attention! Right turn, by the right, quick march. Left, right, left, right.'

With a sigh of relief I halted the squad on the parade ground and reported:

'Leave party all present and correct, Sir.'

I think, in fact I'm sure, he was as much relieved as I was. Of all the sergeant-majors I have served under, and there were many, he was the only one I had any respect for, a real gentleman. The others were all, without exception, inhuman bullies, drunk with power. I make no apologies to anyone for saying so. We boarded the train at the appointed time and, after many sudden jerks, managed to get rolling. Even the train seemed unwilling to leave Rouen and I did not blame it.

After much puffing and blowing, we found ourselves shunted into a siding and it was dark before we got rolling again. In northern France at this time the railways were unbelievably congested; hours and even days sometimes, were spent in sidings and even when we were on the move, we frequently found ourselves in the middle of a queue of twenty or more trains, crawling forwards a hundred or so yards at a time.

At daybreak, we were stationary somewhere in the country and, as was our custom, most of us got down on to the track to stretch our legs. Moving forward, as all good soldiers are taught to do, we made a bee-line for the engine with high hopes of obtaining some hot water in our all-purpose dixies, not that we had any intention of shaving. No, it was breakfast time and, since troop trains out here were composed of an odd assortment of cattle-trucks, we were not blessed with a restaurant-car. We would have to make do with a hot cuppa, if our luck was in. We knew the drill by habit, underneath the foot-plate there's a small pipe that always appears to be dripping. If the elderly driver was in a friendly mood he would pull a small handle or turn a tap or something, which resulted in a burst of steam that made the thirsty soldier-boy withdraw his hand at the double and spill the few drops he had collected in his dixie. The few bursts that followed though were sufficient for his immediate needs. If on the other hand, the old chap on the foot-plate had had a row with his better-half before coming on duty and was not co-operative we would try the next train up the line, time was of no importance; we could be here for hours. On these tantalizing and exasperating journeys one cannot fail to observe the different behaviour of the French troop-train drivers. A few were exceedingly helpful; others appeared to be totally deaf, maybe they were, ignoring all our gestures. Others simply glared at you like the cows grazing by the track, totally uninterested. Still, I have no doubt they all have their own particular worries; who hasn't?

It was dark when I detrained at a rail-head, somewhere in Belgium they said it was. I enquired the whereabouts of my battalion but no one had ever heard of the 'Hood', in fact they had never heard of the Royal Naval Division. One group thought I was stone crackers, a bloke in khaki uniform looking for the Navy so far inland. After traipsing about for hours, or so it seemed, I decided to wait until daylight. Even if someone had a faint idea of which direction I should take, I doubted if I could have found my way in such darkness. I found a fairly comfortable barn and settled down for the night being far too tired to do any more roaming about.

I was up and about at the crack of dawn and made a bee-line trek to a group of ruins nearby and joined a small party of marching men. I enquired as we went along if they had any knowledge of the whereabouts of the Royal Naval Division but none of those I had spoken to, had. Someone suggested that I should ask the sergeant at the cookhouse we were approaching; he might be able to help me. The mention of cook-house was music to my ears; with the exception of a few Huntley and Palmer's biscuits, I had had nothing to eat since leaving Rouen. The sergeant was most sympathetic.

'Join those men at that table over there and eat everything offered to you; then come to me when you have had your fill.'

I didn't need any further instructions. I had a splendid breakfast and was having a smoke when he came to the table and said someone he had spoken to had heard of a Naval crowd in the Neuve Eglise area.

'Come with me outside and I'll show you where to go. See that square tower over in the distance? That's Neuve Eglise. You make for that tower and the best of luck.'

Fully refreshed, I set off full of hope, but, unfortunately the further I walked, the further away the tower seemed to be. I had to keep to the road which endlessly wound its way to nowhere in particular. Sometime later I came across a column of GS wagons halted by the roadside. The officer-in-charge said he had a vague recollection of hearing some mention of the Royal Naval Division, 8th Entrenching Battalion he thought. I said I had never heard of such a battalion; they were certainly not in my crowd. (Incidentally I have never heard of such a battalion since and had never met anyone who had.) He advised me to go back to the railhead, their destination. 'Jump aboard, we're moving off soon.'

Upon arriving at the railhead he spoke to the Rail Transport Officer who in turn, handed me over to another officer with instructions that I was to be sent back to the Royal Naval Division's Depot at Calais. Apparently that's where I should have been sent in the first place.

'You will have to wait for some time. Report to me here when you have had something to eat.'

I was beginning to enjoy the interest that belatedly I was receiving; I'd had two good meals in one day and now I knew exactly where I was bound for. Calais.

CHAPTER TEN

Christmas on the Somme

Wednesday, 29th November

After travelling all night we detrained at Calais at about noon. There was quite a lot of sorting out to do. Batches of men belonging to various regiments were marched off and in the end there were only three Royal Naval Division men left by the side of the track. Where the other two had been, goodness only knows; I certainly didn't. However, as the war had yet to be won and nobody seemed interested in the 'Three Musketeers', we sauntered off and eventually reported at the Royal Naval Division Depot. Our escapades faded into history within minutes of our unannounced arrival. I found myself allocated to a small group, none of whom I knew but a friendly bunch.

Thursday, 30th November

Most of the day was spent collecting equipment including another identification disc, why, I did not know as my original disc was still dangling round my neck as per regulations. The following two days were spent square-bashing at the 'Bull ring' and undergoing gas and tear-shell drill. We had to walk slowly through a covered trench filled with pear-smelling lachrymatory gas to get accustomed to the effect on our eyes when not wearing a mask; then again and again through another cloud of much stronger gas wearing our masks. The result; everyone coughing, spitting and crying their eyes out for quite a time. I felt like a new recruit again but what or how you feel in the forces does not matter any more.

Sunday, 3rd December

A short, but brisk march brought our party to the station. Those of us who were fully blooded by now were fighting fit again and fully aware of the troubles and trials that awaited us at the end of the journey, and yet for some inexplicable reason I was not sorry to be going back to the forward area. I longed for the friendship of real men, men that understood what war was all about, to be among men where trust was mutual and everything was shared, the good and the bad, the delights and the sorrows. We were a huge family who honoured our officers and obeyed automatically; we would follow them to Hell if need be and they knew it.

For the majority of our little bunch it is a voyage into the unknown; they have yet to endure their baptism of fire of which they cannot have the slightest inkling which is just as well. I feel sorry for them; it will be an eye-opener but they will get over it like the rest of us have done and those who survive will be proud and able to walk tall when it is all over. How many? That is in God's hands.

We were anxious to get going but had to endure much hanging about until 7 p.m. when things began to move, and then with somewhat indecent haste we were ordered to climb aboard the train of cattle trucks standing in the siding. Once aboard we came under the direction of the Railway Transport Officer. The conducting NCO cleared off pretty sharpish; he had carried out his stint.

Judging by the state of the floor and the stench, it was apparent that this truck had recently been used for the purpose it was originally intended. However, with the doors on both sides wide open, conditions were not too bad. After a while we all settled down, most of us sitting on our packs and a few stretched out on the floor. Not for long though, as the icy wind necessitated closing the doors on the windward side and about midnight whilst still in the siding, the doors on both sides were closed which meant that we were in total darkness. The French beer and wine we had quaffed had to be got rid of; there were no toilet facilities whatsoever, which meant there was a constant struggling to open the sliding doors, but the change of air was appreciated. It was ten o'clock the following morning before we pulled out of the siding. Fifteen hours to go nowhere and even then throughout the whole day we were constantly shunted into one siding after another. Sometime during the following night we found ourselves in yet another siding; someone said it was Rue. Maybe it was but, judging by the time we had been on our way and the freezing cold, it could have been Omsk or Tomsk on the Trans-Siberian railway.

Tuesday, 5th December

It was noon when we finally arrived at Noyelles-sur-Mer. The fifteen-kilometre march to Le Crotoy at the mouth of the Somme was a pleasure after the cramped conditions of the last couple of days. Upon arriving in this very pleasant seaside town, I was much distressed to learn the extent of our casualties. Unlike the Army procedure where men returning to duty after an absence were drafted to Regiments other than their original one, we in the Naval Brigades always returned to our original battalions. This procedure, though welcomed by the men, meant that each individual was constantly reminded of the demise of his friends.

During the month of November, the division had 160 officers and over 1,670 men killed, another 160 officers and 2,377 men wounded. More than three-quarters of these casualties were in the two Naval brigades.

I felt as though I had been abroad for years and had returned home to find the house empty, the family had gone, the nest was empty. I was a stranger in my own battalion. Fortunately, the free and easy routine, the absence of mud and ear-piercing crescendos of the shell-bursts plus the dreaded uncertainty of everything, had worked wonders amongst us survivors. We felt and acted as though we had been reborn. We could not resist gulping the seaside air; it was so fresh, sweet and free. How lovely it was to step out briskly with head held high, to converse with our fellow men quite rationally and to see contentment in their eyes instead of that vague stare. We were living in a world that we had long since forgotten ever existed. To sleep, perchance to dream; to awake to the sound of a church clock instead of the cry 'Stretcher-Bearers'. Oh vision entrancing! And yet, deep down in my heart I was very sad indeed; so few of those young men I was happy to be with that had left Avonmouth on the *Grantully Castle* in February 1915, with only five people on the quayside to bid us 'bon-voyage' and had survived the slaughter on Gallipoli, two thousand miles away, to be present at the muster today less than a hundred miles from home and beauty, never having seen their loved ones again. So many of them lie in the mud swamps of the Ancre.

Wednesday, 20th December

The weather is fine, not warm but summer-like. The daily routine is still happy-go-lucky and the food luxurious compared with the forward area. Our evenings are free, we spend much of our time in the spacious ballroom listening to the band of the Royal Marines, brought over from England to entertain us. I cannot dance but I enjoy watching those that could. Each night an elderly French citizen amuses all those present with his solo performance, not in any sense a dance but extremely intricate foot-shuffles. He has the floor to himself and somehow he manages to keep in step with the band, who join in the applause of the wallflowers as he takes his bow.

As the days roll on we have become accustomed to this way of life. We visit the *estaminets* although our consumption of cognac is strictly limited, not by any official order, but by our purses. Absolutely no danger of any riotous living, but we are enjoying ourselves all the same. Our ignorance of the language beyond a few phrases which apparently amuse the girls but are not suitable for this narrative, does not prevent us trying them out with varying results not always amusing.

Sunday, 24th December

As this is Christmas Eve our only parade is for Church Service. Somehow these services seem to get more interesting as time goes on. The set-up is much the same wherever they are held. I try to be more attentive and pious but when I close my eyes in prayer, my body is at the service but my thoughts wander. Occasionally I hear what the padre is saying but I'm nowhere near him. In the last few moments I have travelled thousands of miles and I am back on the Gallipoli peninsula, actually in contact with my old buddies, discussing the prospect of home leave during a lull in the fighting agreeing unanimously that we are too far away from home and too much involved with Johnnie Turk at the moment; but some day maybe?

The fascinating human brain is a photographic dictionary of events, all jumbled up yet very clear in their meaning, very much like a magic-lantern show. One moment a pleasing picture warms the blood and the heart rejoices, a slight pause and then a picture that makes the blood run cold; the thoughts of a moment ago, totally reversed, pleasure is turned into hatred and the mind is paralysed.

I could feel my heart pounding away at the granite surrounding it as my section rushed forward to a similar piece of scrub-land to that we had just left, but having my comrades on either side of me gave me courage. The singing rain of lead scythes through the human corn with uncanny accuracy. I was too numbed to be afraid; it took some time for me to realise that I was alone. I wondered what all this was about. I could not see any enemy, only my pals lying motionless around me. We had been together for quite a while and I had come to know not just them but their backgrounds; conversations, long forgotten until now, were remembered. Almost every day Sid would tell all those within hearing distance how clever his sister Jean was at knitting; she would never dream of darning a hole in the heel; it was quicker to knit a fresh heel. A pair of mittens was an afternoon's stint; a multi-coloured fair-isle pullover took a little longer and mufflers were knitted by the yard. The one and only parcel Sid ever received contained half-a-dozen pairs of knee-length navy-blue stockings. I suppose Jean thought that as Sid was in the Navy he was dressed as a sailor during his Christmas leave; he would very often wear sea-boots. She was not the only one; but we were sailors in name only, and engaged in military operations.

Although Sid received only one consignment of stockings, I am certain that many such parcels were dispatched. Those thievish swines who handled the mail en route to the troops pillaged most of the parcels. My mother, weekly without fail, sent me a parcel strongly packed and enclosed in a neatly sewn linen jacket, but very few reached me and only one of those that did was intact. They even pinched my nineteenth-birthday cake.

Pat Kelly had often told me that his mother insisted he should always wear his rosary round his neck. 'It will keep you safe,' she said, and there had been dear 'old' Sammy, almost twenty, always up to some devilment and never appreciated by our Chief Petty Officer; he had had many a good hiding for playing truant from school, run away from home, had done a few trips on the Mersey ferry, and then gone back home to yet another tanning. Eventually he had managed to find himself a good, steady job to become the breadwinner of the family. His father was in casual work, more out of work than in, which was common in those days, and may have had something to do with his outrageous temper. Sammy was on the small side, so small in fact I wondered how he had managed to enlist. In those early days of the war the response to the 'Call to Arms' was really overwhelming. The recruiting staff could be, and were, very eclectic. But Sammy's fertile brain was quick on the draw, and he exaggerated a little regarding his sea-service. His stunted stature in no way lessened the height of his character, I am proud to have known him and the other boys who made up my section. Eight out of twelve were now dead after less than five weeks fighting.

During my short furlough at Christmas 1914. I had seen the effect on my mother after my brother's death while serving on HMS *Good Hope* and can visualise the grief the parents back home have to bear. I think it was M.W. Balfe who composed the following lines that more adequately convey my feelings.

The heart bowed down by weight of woe
To weakest hopes will cling;
To thought and impulse while they flow,
That can no comfort bring;
With those exciting scenes will blend,
O'er pleasures pathway thrown,
But memory is the only friend,
That grief can call its own.
The mind will in its worst despair,
Still ponder o'er the past;
On moments of delight that were,
Too beautiful to last.

The stentorian voice of the Chief Petty Officer awakened me from my dream. The Church Service was over and I am amongst the rest of his puppets, nicely lined up on the roadway now much comforted. The Padre had reminded us that the good God was on our side. He is certainly on my side but, for the life of me, I don't understand why. After some time we were dismissed for dinner; lunch for the officers but dinner for the rankers. The usual menu, bully-beef stew, cabbage – or was it some other weed, they all taste alike – and boiled potatoes. Nothing special. We had rather expected a change considering it was Christmas Eve, but in the Army, what you expect and what you get are always at variance. However, it seemed pretty certain that I would not have to spend Christmas Day in the firing line as was my luck last year. The war goes on and someone has to be in the firing line every day, festival or no festival. The awful experience I had last Christmas will haunt me for the rest of my days.

Christmas Day: Monday, 25th December 1916

We paraded in beautiful sunshine at eleven o'clock and marched to the aerodrome some little distance from the town. There were not many civilians about in the streets but those that were gave the conquering heroes an enthusiastic wave as we passed. For a long time now I have known that I am no longer Mother's little angel. I have broken most of the Ten Commandments just trying to keep alive and have been at various times a disciple of 'Old Nick'. There is no need for the Padre to lecture me about purgatory; I've been there. I've seen the fire and gone through it several times, the smell of brimstone is still in my nostrils. I have endured over eighteen months of Hell-fire. No wonder I am cynical most of the time. Even today I cannot make up my mind whether the waving is a patriotic gesture or a sign of relief at our imminent departure.

Punctually is the essence of politeness, so they say. The Military authorities are expert in these matters, except when dishing out the five francs of the many they owe me. If the General condescends to inspect his men before he condemns them to the inevitable slaughter or even if a Petty Officer assembles a fatigue party, the Poor Bloody Infantry are always on parade hours before the event and consequently, they arrive at the appointed venue much ahead of time. Today we waited two hours outside the hangars at the aerodrome before the huge doors were opened, revealing several long lines of trestle tables to which we were eventually allocated. They reminded me of the only school treat I had been privileged to attend. At close intervals on the well-scrubbed tables were placed an apple and a packet of ten, Army-issue cigarettes. This well-meant display invited all the strategy of musical chairs when the order to sit down was given. As is usual in all movements in the Services, one is never in the correct position at the first attempt. All ranks knew that there would be considerable shuffling about before the final positioning was accomplished. The greedy ones quietly pocketed the buckshee fags at the first sitting which resulted in some of the wide-boys having several packets and some little doggies having none.

I didn't bother to enquire who it was that was responsible for the table arrangements; he must have been a first-day rookie, to leave cigarettes lying about was inviting trouble. But it was Christmas Day, a day to give not to take away. Had not the Padre only yesterday told us forgiving was a noble virtue, so all was forgiven just this once, for the Padre's peace of mind.

We were many miles from the fighting line but after another hour or so, the lads were by now rather impatient, to say the least. Their continuous banging of their billy-cans on the tables emulated a minor bombardment and one had to take evasive measures from the hail of apple cores; they were much too sour to eat anyway. A rumour was circulating that one of the cooks had told somebody that the dinner would be ready in half-an-hour and the din ceased a little, probably not because of the good news but from sheer exhaustion. At four o'clock a prolonged shriek of a whistle meant that something special was about to be announced, and, when the officer had satisfied himself that his authority had been recognised, he said in a very apologetic tone that he was extremely sorry for the delay but it had been unavoidable: the fresh meat had been boiling since breakfast-time but was still quite tough – another half-hour might do the trick. All and sundry were in no mood for further delay. 'Dish out the stuff now,' was the consensus. Well, we asked for it and we got it; a good measure of potato stew, jackets included, cabbage that looked like seaweed and tasted like it and small chunks of the aforementioned fresh meat. It may have been fresh before hostilities began but it was certainly not fresh now, nor was it beef or mutton. I hadn't noticed any travelling circuses in the neighbourhood but if there were, I'm afraid a couple of their star attractions must have gone astray. Needless to mention, that concluded the meals for the day.

Wednesday, 27th December

After a more or less day off yesterday, we vacated Le Crotoy and marched to St Quentin a short distance further up the coast, the 'Drake' battalion were to take our place at Le Crotoy; it was their turn for a seaside holiday and they had certainly earned it.

Our training here was in no way strenuous; it was mostly route marching and battalion operations and getting used to be soldiers instead of tourists. The complete change away from the fighting had done us the world of good, we were gradually becoming fighting men again. That's why we were on foreign soil, nicely fattened up and ready for slaughter. That's what war is all about and what we soldiers are trained for and expected to do. All the same we were sorry to leave Le Crotoy; we had been treated as tourists by the inhabitants, but all good things must inevitably come to an end.

Monday, 1st January 1917

A new year and a more rigorous programme. We marched to Vercourt for brigade operations which included forced marches that were very exhausting. Leaving our billets at six o'clock in the morning we were almost worn out by the time we arrived back at seven in the evening. These brigade operations involve all four battalions in all sorts of manoeuvres every other day during our stay at St Quentin. Fortunately the weather is not too bad which is quite a change.

Saturday, 13th January

Apparently our holiday is over. Since the beginning of the New Year the weather has been fairly dry but cold but during the night it began to rain and it was still pouring down as we began our march back to the Inferno. For some reason we seemed to be in a hurry and moved at a quicker pace than our normal two-and-a-half miles per hour. Even so, it was late afternoon when we marched into the village of Laviers, our resting place for the night. My aching feet seem to tell me we have trudged at least thirty-two kilometres in the pouring rain.

Sunday, 14th January

The rain had turned to snow and there was a thick carpet on the ground when we resumed our march. At a rough guess, I would estimate that the four companies of a battalion marching in column of fours would stretch for about four hundred yards, so that as I was in 'C' Company there were two-and-a-half companies ahead of my section treading the still falling snow into a slippery, freezing slush making the going extremely arduous. It was still snowing when we reached Agenvillers and settled down for the night, having covered about twenty-four kilometres.

Monday, 15th January

The snow was falling heavily as we continued our way back to the danger zone but we were getting used to the hard going by now. Marching in such atrocious weather does not boost one's morale, hardened as we are. Still, it wasn't anyone's fault; it was just rough luck and we had to make the best of it. There is nothing like a bit of singing while on the march and every man-jack joining in to cheer things up, especially when approaching a village, and there have been many sing-songs. We don't need any prompting, we automatically become parade soldiers.

Tired and weary though we were, we braced ourselves up, demonstrating to the French inhabitants and any troops that happened to be about, that the Royal Naval Division men could march as well as any others. They had proved that we were second to none where fighting was concerned. The Commander-in-Chief, Sir Douglas Haig, had said so in his address to the division after the Ancre battle: we had captured more ground and taken more prisoners in any single day's fighting, hitherto on the Western

Mud.

Front. We were top of the class and proud of it.

The snow was still falling as we slithered into the sleepy village of Fienvillers at the end of our thirty-odd kilometre saunter.

Tuesday, 16th January

The snow was still falling even more heavily at breakfast-time. Whether because of this or whether someone thought we needed a rest, there were no parades except 'feet inspection' which always aroused much coarse banter.

Wednesday, 17th January

Off again. It's still snowing. We are not the only troops on the move, which means we are nearing the fighting zone. The roads are congested with moving artillery of all shapes and sizes and going in all directions. Our column was held up many times; most unusual in the back areas. However we managed to arrive at our destination just outside the village, le Val-de-Maison. Instead of flopping down in broken-down houses or barns, we came to rest on a wide open space where quite a few bell-tents were standing in about a foot of snow. I don't know how the other companies fared but my mob had to erect their tents before settling down for the night. The erecting of a single bell-tent is not as easy as it looks at the best of times, but to get several of them in proper alignment acceptable to the officer-in-charge on a carpet of snow with a gale blowing severely tests the tempers of all concerned, and that this time included the officer, even though he was the best of a highly respected bunch we were fortunate to be honoured with. The job of clearing the snow from inside the tent was an arduous task as the frozen ropes had severely lacerated our hands, but it was a task that had to be done before anything else. The piping-hot stew that followed certainly warmed our bodies and only if we could have dried our uniforms, our rest overnight would have been much more comfortable than it was but we had by now, given up any hope of comfort at any time.

Thursday, 18th January

Still snowing as heavily as ever. Will it ever stop? No parades today; practically the whole of the day was spent sheltering in our tent. Our only excursions outside were to the field-kitchens to scrounge something hot to eat and drink. The condensation inside was almost unbearable.

Friday, 19th January

The heavens have run short of snow: the first dry morning for a week. It was perishing cold when we paraded to begin another route march wondering how far it would be this time. We were actually anxious to get moving and warmed up. For some reason or other we were kept hanging about the whole of the forenoon and when we eventually moved off we only marched a little way before we were halted by the roadside. However the brisk march had warmed us up. Our stay here was not long. A fleet of lorries drew up alongside and we were ordered to jump aboard the nearest vehicle. After several starts we were on our way, destination unknown. We were presumably going somewhere and seemed to be in a devilish hurry to get to where it was. The minor roads in France were not made for the traffic they were obliged to carry in war-time and consequently it was questionable if the old adage, 'A bad ride is better than a good walk' had any truth in it. Every pot-hole brought a painful jar and the lorry's springs, if they ever had any, lost whatever resilience they originally had. Frozen stiff, cramped and bruised all over, we were dumped by the roadside in the darkness at a place that went by the name of Lancashire Dump, somewhere behind Thiepval I think, and we remained there all night. We are under no delusions about being back in the war again. It was a lousy, miserable night.

Saturday, 20th January

At daybreak we were on the move again. Soon after winding our way through the ruins of Authuille, I think, we crossed the flooded marshes of the Ancre and reached what was left of the village of Hamel. We had a short rest for breakfast and then went up the Beaucourt road to what had been the German front line before our attack on 13th November. We took up our position in reserve here and I felt I was back home again knowing my way about here so well. Some of Jerry's heavy stuff welcomed our homecoming which was to be expected as this had been his homeland for years until we cleared him out.

Sunday, 21st January

I am now Number One of a Lewis gun team, that is the chap that pulls – no, that's not correct – who presses the trigger that does the damage. As soon as it was dark enough for us to go forward, we went over the top with the digging party that were to dig what we called a jumping-off trench, and I took up my position a little ahead of them to deter any enemy interference with the job on hand. The advantage of these very shallow trenches, actually joining up a series of shell-holes, reduces the distance that the leading troops in the coming attack will have to cover when the artillery barrage creeps forward from the enemy's front line. The Engineers had been out there and laid a thin white tape to show the lads where to dig. Just before dawn the working party withdrew to our own lines and then to their position in reserve. I withdrew my gun-team to the newly dug trench and occupied it until the very last moment before rejoining the working party. There is always the possibility of the enemy patrols occupying the partially dug trench if we evacuate it too soon. When we were all safely back, the infantry holding the line would replace the barbed wire in the gaps that had been made for us. This digging business is the nightly routine in our sector. If there is no attack pending, the reserves with the men holding the line will be out in front repairing our barbed wire or maybe adding to it, or lugging ammunition about; there's never a dull moment. Officially, the communique tells the folks back home that 'All is quiet on the Western Front'. It's never, never quiet out here; it's banging and crashing all the time.

Friday, 26th January

Late in the evening we were relieved by the Royal Fusiliers and made our way back to Forceville, arriving at 4 a.m. on the 27th. We were on the move again at 11 a.m. to the village of Arqueves. It was only a short distance but the roads were so congested that we finally reached our billets at 6 p.m. Orders were given that we were to clean ourselves up, buttons shining, boots dubbined and facial growth removed as parade would be in one hour's time. That was plenty of time if we had any 'Soldier's Friend' or Dubbin but we had neither. Our buttons were polished with God's earth and a bucket of filthy water made our boots look as though they had been dubbined while they were still wet. Punctually at seven o'clock we were on parade for inspection, clean as new pins. My platoon officer, Lieutenant Jacobs, a really charming fellow by any standards, gazed first at my boots, then my buttons and, finally my face with the aid of an almost run-down torch. Maybe my slight smile distracted him as the next man to me was not so lucky.

'Take this man's name, Petty Officer.'

And so the farce continued along the line. 'To those about to die, make sure your face is clean.' On the whole, our stay in this sorely battered village was easy going. There were the usual fatigues of course; we were beasts of burden mostly carrying all manner of requirements of war from one dump to another similar one. In all probability another fatigue party would carry it back again but it kept the troops busy and took our minds off the coming attack. Our meals were always piping hot for a change and we were able to eat them in peace. The menu never changed but if you were at the end of the queue, you might get a more solid ladleful from the bottom of the dixie.

CHAPTER ELEVEN

Offensive at Beaucourt

Friday, 2nd February

Our week's 'rest' out of the forward zone trenches had come to an end. We were conveyed by London General Omnibus, 'B' type buses to Mesnil, via Lealvillers, Varennes and Hedauville. Immediately upon arrival we moved forward and entered a communication trench just beyond Hamel to shelter from the heavy shelling. Time and time again we were halted as quite a lot of shells appeared to be falling just ahead of us, making progress extremely erratic. After sheltering here for quite some time the shelling eased a little and, taking advantage of this, we moved forward trying to hurry, but not really managing very well owing to the direct hits on this already battered communication trench. About fifty yards of it had ceased to exist and the appalling scene made me feel sick; there were dead and dying everywhere. Even though it was broad daylight we were forced to make our way over the top in the open, a suicidal move but the only option available – a leap-frog movement in and out of the repulsive intermingled and slimy shell craters.

The whole of the Ancre valley is a filthy quagmire. Ice had formed on the stagnant water but gave way under our weight. Balance lost, we clambered out of the craters on all fours to plunge into the next, and the next. After years of constant shelling there's not a yard of even ground anywhere in the valley. At the opening of the Somme offensive on 1st July last year our troops advanced over this ground but were repulsed; several attempts were made later with the same result. The enemy, fully aware of the strategic value of this desolate morass, had resisted all attempts to dislodge him until we finally drove him out on 13th November. He probably knows it was our mob who had ousted him on that day and he has since endeavoured to make our occupation untenable.

The shelling continues, each salvo putting some poor old blighter out of his misery without a murmur. Later on the gleaners may gather his remains in a sack; quite a number are blown to pieces every hour and will not have a Christian burial as we know it. They will be listed as 'missing'. What a cruel cold-blooded tag for some son whose mother in the months or even years ahead will cling to the hope that he may turn up somewhere. Maybe he has been taken prisoner; maybe she will have news of him from a prisoner-of-war camp. 'No news is good news', it is said, but not for the missing out here. I have no spiritualistic notions as far as I know, but there are moments when I wonder that, if it were possible to converse with any of my departed pals, what their answer would be to my question, 'Is all this pain and suffering getting us anywhere?' I know it is impossible to give a direct answer; after all, what is pain, what is suffering? It's all a matter of degree, physical and mental. These afflictions are with us every day of our lives and the people back home, miles away from the horrors of war, are maybe suffering more than we are for unseen tears and sorrows are the deepest. Men are born to die; the time and place is of no consequence. Each breath of life we take or give, leaves us less of life to live. Providence is our only hope as the shells continue to reap their harvest.

A thoroughly exhausted and disorganised bunch eventually reached a line comprised of shell-holes linked together by a shallow trench. Several of these craters were quite deep and an attempt had been made to give some covering overhead. It was to one of these cubby-holes that I and the other surviving NCOs were summoned for our final briefing. We were told that we were to attack and capture the two lines of trenches immediately in front of us at eleven o'clock – a minor operation which would take only eight minutes to complete. Lieutenant Jacobs produced several photographs that had been taken at three o'clock this afternoon by a low flying aeroplane. They were very dark, more like negatives than prints. However, there were distinct markings that he explained were machine-gun posts; there was also a smaller earthwork probably occupied by a single gun and two or three men over on our left flank beyond the Baillescourt-Beaucourt road. There were more clearly defined earthworks than most of the other markings but they were not on our patch; the 'Hawke' battalion on our left would deal with that side of the road. On our right flank there were several ill-defined posts and the capture of these would mean that the platoon on that flank would have to turn half-right as the river at this point takes a sharp right-angle bend. If these posts were not captured they would play havoc with our line of communication and make our position intolerable.

To carry out such a movement in daylight would be very complicated, to attempt it in the dark could be disastrous. As soon as we had consolidated our position in the captured second trench, an NCO and two men were to go forward and raid the Baillescourt Farm some five hundred or so yards further on, and bring back all the documents they could find. A DCM would be awarded if the raid was successful. Leading Seaman Charlton who was the senior NCO present, volunteered and I was to keep him covered with my gun-team. After the briefing he and I discussed our tactics with our respective gun teams and almost at once we began our move forward. It was very dark, about 6 p.m. I should think. Most of the way we were sheltered in a communication trench running towards the firing line but time and time again we had to traverse the open ground where the trench ceased to exist. We had to go through the ruins of Beaucourt at the double, a section at a time, as Jerry seemed to be concentrating his fire on the road.

By eight o'clock we were in our assembly trench, a line of shell-holes linked together by a shallow trench affording very little cover. With three hours to wait before the attack we made ourselves as comfortable as we could in the circumstances. The night was clear but a keen frost tested our endurance. Exercise was out of the question. We were in an advanced position and three hours is a very long time in such a precarious position. As the time passed the freezing conditions seemed to partially paralyse the brain and all sorts of events, long since forgotten, came to life in a topsy-turvy sequence and vied with each other for prominence. Maybe it was a God-send to keep our minds off the coming carnage. We knew our attack was a local affair, a trench to trench leap on a very narrow frontage by three companies of the 'Hood' and three from the 'Hawke'. The four companies in the centre were to thrust forward in two waves; the flanks, on a lesser frontage, were to be dealt with by the other two companies.

Our object was to capture the remainder of the ridge which would give us command of Grandcourt on the other side of the river, a key position of the enemy's defensive line. Because of the importance of the ridge, no advance was to be attempted on either side of us. We were in no doubt as to the magnitude of the opposition that would be hauled against us during the attack and the difficulty we would experience in consolidating our gains. At eleven o'clock in brilliant moonlight the barrage opened up. We went forward up the rising ground following closely behind the creeping barrage; the ground on our right flank fell sharply towards the river. After advancing some considerable distance we were ordered to dig in. This order confused me. Where were the trenches we were to capture? However, I took my gun-team forward about thirty yards to give cover to the men who were to dig in. I could hear the ringing noises of their entrenching tools on the frozen ground. Whilst here I was joined by Petty Officer Egdell who was in charge of the company's Lewis guns. He was also company quartermaster. What he was doing here baffled me as his job was to see that we received our rations, but I was pleased to see him.

Fully satisfied that my gun was effectively positioned, he and I went forward to reconnoitre and, to our amazement found ourselves plodging about in the marshes. Retracing our movements, we scrambled back up the steep slope and rejoined my gun-team. Up to now we had not met with much opposition but things were livening up. The artillery were still pounding away some distance to our left but machine-gun fire was coming from all directions, so heavily that we were forced to lie low.

After a while the men that we were covering began to move away from us. PO Egdell set off towards them to ascertain what was really happening. I withdrew my team to the place where the men had been trying to dig in. A short burst of machine-gun fire helped us on our way and I found myself in a shell-hole with Petty Officer

Price and his gun-team. How long he had been there I did not know; like me, he could not understand what was happening and, having told him where Egdell and I had been and since Egdell had gone in search of the others, I was going in search of him. Two hand-grenades landed very close and this decided us that we were not welcome here. We agreed to move at once, and I collected my gun team who were in a nearby crater.

The moment we began to move we were fired upon from a very close range from behind as was the machine-gun burst previously. I set off again with PO Price following about ten yards behind with his team. I took my direction from the partly-dug trench and realised that I was walking almost parallel with the river which shone in the moonlight. Whether on account of the sloping nature of the ground or because the whole of the attacking force had erroneously turned half-right instead of only the right flank platoon doing this, we had ended up on an alignment parallel with, instead of at right-angles to, the river.

I had by now collected another gun-crew. PO Price had caught up with us and all three teams were cogitating on what our next move should be when we were rudely disturbed by a shower of hand-grenades all round us. Most of us saw a party of about a dozen men approaching from our rear and thought they were our own men coming to our aid; until they lobbed their grenades at us. My Number One, always on the alert as usual, let off half a magazine into them as they disappeared down the slope but, unfortunately several of our parties were killed. As we were in separate shell-holes my party escaped with only one man rather badly wounded. Price called out that he was OK but he had several casualties. I suggested that we should move at once but he refused to budge so I moved with my gun-team towards where I thought our men should be.

We had gone about twenty yards or so when there was a hellish crash near the spot we had a few moments ago been resting. It was much too heavy to be grenades and there were several shells falling around at the time. I never saw PO Price again but I did meet up with PO Egdell some minutes later and went with him along the crest of the ridge to the Beaucourt-Baillescourt road, the extreme left flank of the 'Hoods' frontage, where I took up a position with my own and Leading Seaman Charlton's gun-teams. He had been wounded in the knee, someone said.

It was a lovely position, looking down now instead of always having to look upwards to the higher ground. I could see Baillescourt Farm quite clearly about six hundred yards ahead to the right of the road but could not see any earthworks between our position and the farm. Everyone was trying to dig themselves in. The severe frosts of the last month or so had made the ground cast-iron hard and our entrenching tools were practically useless but some sort of a defensive trench had to be made before dawn. The occasional shell crater helped a little but it was still a heart-breaking task. As there had been no attack on either flank we could expect a rude awakening when Jerry had sorted himself out. All the Kaiser's horses and all the Kaiser's men would be thrown at us – a handful of men in khaki with naval pay, ratings and customs, perched on top of an important ridge that commanded the village of Grandcourt.

Expecting the inevitable counter-attack at any moment, we made frantic efforts to join up our individual slit trenches. Several times during the hours of darkness, we had to deal with small groups of the enemy coming towards us from the rear. Because we had somehow lost direction and had veered to the right during our advance, these enemy troops had been missed but, now we are in correct alignment but not actually in touch with the 'Hawke' battalion on our left. All night long there had been considerable activity behind us on both flanks. It appeared to me that the enemy were trying to prevent our supporting troops reaching us from Beaucourt and that our chaps were attempting to come forward to fill the gap on our left between the 'Hawke' and the 'Hood'. The road at this point as it went over the crest of the ridge had been cut out of the sloping ground, creating a five or six feet drop on the high side. I positioned one of my guns on this higher ground to protect our flank; the others I kept as near to the roadway as possible because the elevation gave me an uninterrupted field of fire for at least a mile or so ahead.

Sunday, 4th February

At breakfast-time everything appeared to be under control. A working party, from the Worcestershire Pioneer battalion I believe, had deposited a good stock of picks and shovels quite close to the roadway some distance behind us but within easy reach and we were able to get on with our consolidation unmolested in the sunshine. Revelling in the sudden warmth and intrigued by the fantastic will-o'-the-wisp patterns of the dispersing haze in the valley, I was amazed to observe an officer and about thirty of our men, surrendering on our extreme right. PO Egdell grabbed one of my guns and ran some distance along the line and emptied a full magazine in their direction but they continued on their way apparently unmolested for another five minutes before they were lost to my view.

I do not know the circumstances in which the officer and his men were in, what I do know is that I and many others were in that area during the night and were subjected to persistent bombing and close range firing. There is no doubt in my mind that the surrender was involuntary.

As the morning wore on my position on the crest became, to me, intolerable as we were being subjected to an incessant stream of bullets singing much too close overhead from somewhere behind us. I decided to advance my position about fifteen yards down the slope beyond the ridge. Ringing in my ears was the advice given me by Colonel B.C. Freyberg (later General Lord Freyberg VC) when he promoted me on 31st January to Able Seaman Higher Grade.

'Never be afraid to make a decision. Weigh up the facts as you know them before you decide but, once having made your decision, stick to it.'

After my move was completed I sent young Smithy, my runner, back to the line to notify my company commander Burnett, of my new position and the reason for it. It was much later in the day that I was told that the Machine-gun Company, well behind us, were keeping up a barrage beyond us on account of the gap between us and the 'Hawke'.

At about four in the afternoon, heavy fighting was in progress some distance away on our extreme left. We were not involved but of course, kept a sharp look-out in case. My experience in the trenches on Gallipoli was that if firing broke out on any part of the line, it inevitably spread along the whole line, but the conditions of the fighting out there were vastly different. The full extent of the firing line was less than four miles whereas out here it stretches from the sea to the Swiss border. The opposing lines are hundreds of yards apart and very seldom seen; on Gallipoli they were always seen and often not more than ten yards separated the two firing lines. In fact one stretch of our line, aptly named 'Eastern birdcage', had a sloping roof of several frames of netting-wire as a shield against the constant rain of hand-grenades.

Throughout the daylight hours there were many minor attacks and much shelling in front and behind our position. Both our flanks were in the air. Consequently we were subjected to all sorts of hostility – grenades, rifle-fire and shells coming from all directions – which prevented our support troops from coming to our aid. At about 7 p.m. a small party from the 'Drake' battalion reached our line and almost at once we were counter-attacked in force. Time and time again we beat them off but on they came again and again after a short pause, however, our line held and we were very thankful to have had a few 'Drakes' amongst us.

As the hours passed, the enemy increased his shelling immediately behind us, obviously endeavouring to prevent any help reaching us. Another small batch of men reached us a few minutes before he attacked again in force, but those of the 'Drakes' that were following must have suffered many casualties during the blanket shelling of the road and the only communication trench from Beaucourt.

The counter-attacking went on for four hours and sometime during the night I was amazed to see a German officer on the roadway only a couple of yards in front of me. How he had managed to get so near puzzled me as my eight Lewis guns were firing incessantly. No one could possibly survive such concentrated fire. He must have approached from the higher ground on the other side of the road which was dead ground to our line of fire, and even so he must have crawled. I didn't have to take aim, because he was so near. My revolver shot caused him to fall into our shell-hole and, in doing so, put two of my guns temporarily out of action. The Lewis gun is an extremely fickle piece of mechanism; a speck of dust on the feed-arm is sufficient to render it useless until cleared. The ten degrees of frost we were enduring did not make things any easier. The German officer had been carrying a brand new rifle, with a serrated bayonet, contrary to all rules and regulations. I handed over the rifle but ran the risk of keeping the saw-bayonet as a souvenir. A close friend of mine, actually a neighbour and a boozing pal of my father, granted compassionate leave to sort out his family trouble some time later, 'borrowed' it without my knowledge, and that was the last I saw of my souvenir. Nemesis? I learned much later that he was seen brandishing it in the village pub looking for the man who was the cause of his trouble.

During a lull I sent my runner back to the line to report that I had accepted most of the ammunition brought up by the Pioneer battalion, forty-thousand rounds of it. One of my men had managed to get hold of an ex-petrol can of water, but unfortunately it was no longer water; it was solid ice. The sporadic firing went on all through the night with varying intensity.

Monday, 5th February

As dawn broke the intensity of the numerous counter-attacks was revealed by the number of dead lying out in front. It had been a very hectic night. The transient gleam from the bursting shells revealed figures coming towards us and the ensuing darkness made giants of them all; they seemed to be indestructible. Anything, large or small, approaching me in the gloom was an enemy; a menace and self-preservation urged me to swing my gun from side to side spraying the phantoms, only pausing to re-load with another magazine of forty-seven rounds. Normally, I would not have to do any firing but my chaps had been at it almost continuously for two days. When one feels his life is threatened it is surprising the amount of energy that can be commanded only for it to flit away the moment the imminent danger is passed.

Many times during the night I had to struggle to prevent my eyelids closing with only partial success but my brain was awake and fear stoked up my mind. I was fully conscious of what was happening. In the dim, dawn light, the sun not yet visible, my men were trying to prise pieces of ice from the petrol can with their bayonets and sharing the results of their labours. Our hands were so cold that the ice showed no signs of melting.

At about seven o'clock in the morning, Sub-Lieutenant Holland crawled out to my position to give me the congratulations of our company commander, Lieutenant-Commander Burnett. I passed on the message to my scattered gun-crews quite loudly I confess. I wanted them all to hear as we had been somewhat isolated from the men in the front line practically throughout the whole operation. The half-a-dozen words of appreciation put new life into us all. While I was chatting with the officer, my runner, young Smithy, who had eyes as keen as a hawk's, pointed out a considerable formation of Germans apparently crossing the river and the marshes now frozen hard, about seven or eight hundred yards ahead of us but quite some distance to our right. It appeared that there was some dead ground on our side of the river as the head of the column was observed seemingly making for Baillescourt Farm. It was doubtful if they were within our effective range. A road ran from the river and in front of the farm. If they were using that road, and their formation told us they were, we would have the whole column broadside on very soon. By their formation it was obvious that they were not intending to attack. They seemed unaware that the crest of the ridge was in our hands. I could not understand this as only a few hours ago we had been attacked repeatedly from this direction. I felt certain that, if we waited a little while, they would be broadside on and a sitting target for my eight Lewis guns who could and would, make short work of them. Sub-Lieutenant Holland was of the same mind. He crawled back to our line to report to our company commander and to suggest that the infantrymen hold their fire until we opened up with our machine-guns. As no further orders came I assumed that our plan had been accepted and I instructed my teams to await my signal. It seemed an eternity before I was satisfied that we had a perfect target; actually it was only a few minutes. I fired the first burst; seconds later our artillery blasted Baillescourt Farm for about five minutes.

When the smoke cleared there were no signs of any movement. Sub-Lieutenant Holland appeared with more congratulations from the commander. I was instructed to take a small party forward to gather as much material as possible from the dead lying immediately in front, the price they had paid for their repeated counter-attacks. Venturing forward for about fifty yards we rummaged about for maybe ten minutes or so gathering what we could unmolested and were almost back in our own shell-holes when a short burst of machine gun from the direction of our own front line wounded three of another party only a few yards to our left who were returning from a similar mission. Some little time later on I was informed that Lieutenant Commander Burnett had been wounded in the elbow and that Sub-Lieutenant Jacobs had been killed.

CHAPTER TWELVE

Gavrelles

Tuesday, 6th February

In the early hours we were relieved by the Honorable Artillery Company. On handing over my post to an officer, it was customary to explain the outlay of the position, the officer said that he did not envy us our journey back as the Jerries had given them a bashing coming up. 'We should have relieved you chaps hours ago'. We talked of the recent happenings in front of the farm and the vulnerability of the left flank. To the best of my knowledge, there was still a gap on the other side of the road. As I was about to take my leave, he said he felt so bally hungry he could eat a tin of jam raw.

The journey to the rear was a nightmare, as I had been told it would be. There was no shelter at all over the newly captured open ground. The road to Beaucourt was a graveyard of many of the ration parties that had attempted to get through to us. Dixies that once held that much needed precious hot stew were perforated and scattered all over the place, intermingled with broken boxes of ammunition, picks and shovels. When we reached the ruins of the village, it was a dreadful sight: mutilated bodies of men, horses and mules everywhere among which we had to shelter while waiting a chance to run the gauntlet around the spot known to us as 'suicide corner' where the road turns sharply to go down the hill to Hamel. This road, the only one, and the only way in or out of the area of our attack, had been in enemy hands for years and as there was no fighting taking place on either flank, they were free to concentrate all their fire on this narrow strip of activity. Some small groups managed to get beyond the ruins without serious loss but others were not so fortunate.

I had lost several men during the battle and the subsequent holding of the captured ground which was to be expected but having fought continuously for over two days when it was supposed to take only eight minutes, it was most distressing to have to tread over the bodies of one's pals who had fought so courageously and were almost in sight of a few days' rest in comparative safety. It was for me to decide which of my survivors would run the gauntlet, and when. Fortunately, by dispatching three or four at varying intervals we were all able to be at the muster, a very sorrowful one as usual, when we eventually reached Lancashire Dump, a short distance to the rear but still within artillery range. A welcome hot meal awaited us, our first meal of any sort for over three days.

After the usual hour or two of hanging about we boarded some buses that had just arrived and journeyed to Forceville, in the Acheux area.

Wednesday, 7th February

We were told officially that two patrols from the 'Howe' battalion had entered Grandcourt during the night of the 5th/6th and reported it deserted. At breakfast time the 2nd Royal Marines entered the place and confirmed the enemy retirement. Grandcourt was the first place of any importance to be abandoned by the German army on the Western Front and was the beginning of the general retreat to the well-prepared Hindenburg Line.

There were no parades at all today, which was just as well. We were really in a sorry plight and once we sat down, the majority of us did not have enough energy to get up again. I managed to take off my boots after a struggle and found a few of my toes had burst at the tips looking not unlike the gaping mouths of dead fish. I bandaged my feet as best as I could with pieces of not very clean rag but cleaner than my wet, stinking, part-worn socks. Using the leg part of my socks to keep the rags in place I was ready to enjoy a good night's rest. What a hope! As soon as I began to thaw out I could not prevent my feet rising as though they were trying to escape from my legs. The excruciating pain was almost unbearable but there was nothing I could do, or anyone else. Although thoroughly exhausted, sleep evaded me.

Thursday, 8th February

At breakfast time I decided that I must report sick at the First Aid Post some distance down the road from our barn. The problem was how to get there. My boots were frozen stiff, try as I may, I could not get my hands inside them to straighten out the kinks. I tried for some time to make the uppers pliable but to no avail. I pinched a sandbag and wrapped it around the foot that was most painful and, with my boots tied by the laces, slung round my neck, I began my slow, agonizing trek, which reminded me of our final trek from the firing-line to 'V' beach during the last hour of the Gallipoli campaign. On that occasion the sandbags were to lessen the noise of our footsteps but this morning, it was Hobson's choice.

There were quite a few reporting sick, when it came to my turn to be attended to the Medical Officer, who recognised me as an 'old hand' said jokingly:

'Where the hell have you been?'

I explained that during the night of the 3rd/4th I had been wallowing in the swamps of the Ancre and since then I had been getting some of my own back on the Jerries with the aid of a few Lewis guns.

'You chaps put up a damned good show, I have heard that Petty Officer Egdell has been recommended for the Distinguished Conduct Medal.'

He patched me up, wished me 'Good Luck', and I was carried away with my boots still dangling round my neck, to a waiting lorry. More cases came aboard and, when it was somewhat crowded, we were whisked away to Clayfair Farm hospital, situated in what was known to us as 'the Corps Rest Station'. Of its whereabouts behind the line I haven't the remotest idea. After further examination and treatment, I was allocated to a bell tent and put to bed, three hard boards on two low trestles plus a palliasse, made the bed comfortable. With hot stew inside me, it was home from home compared with the conditions of late. The male orderlies were most considerate at all times of the day and night. It was three weeks before I was able to get my boots on, now nicely thawed out and cleaned, and enjoyed the exercise I sorely needed.

Tuesday, 6th March

I was discharged from hospital today and was told that my battalion was somewhere in the Pozières area. I had an idea of where Pozières was, but no idea of where I was other than the name of the hospital. I had been dumped here a month or so ago but had not been able to venture more than a few yards from my tent. Everyone seemed to be coming or going all the time, there was no opportunity to find out anything, for we were all in the same boat. I didn't expect a personal escort but, as this was the 'Corps' rest station, I had expected to be given some definite directions as to how and where I could reach my battalion. It was not one of my lucky days; all those to whom I spoke with, and there were many, could not help in any way.

I knew that Pozières was on the road from Albert to Bapaume so I decided to cadge a lift on any vehicle going in that direction. I had to walk for quite a while before I came across a stationary convoy on a main road. On enquiry, I was told that they were bound for Albert. That would do quite nicely, I thought, and promptly climbed aboard the nearest lorry as the convoy was moving off in the direction that I had come from.

After a while I could see in the distance the 'Golden Virgin' hanging perilously from the two hundred and odd feet tower of the Basilique Notre Dame de Brebières. She had hung this way since 15th January 1915.* The convoy came to a standstill when its head reached the church which meant that, as I was in the last lorry, I had some distance to walk before entering Albert from whence I would trek towards Bapaume.

After ambling along for about half a mile I managed to get a lift as far as the outskirts of La Boisselle and was able to scrounge something to eat and drink there. I was also able to get confirmation of the whereabouts of the Royal Naval Division who were evidently at Springfield Camp, Pozières. Actually it turned out that they were nearer Ovillers in reserve on the Bapaume front, and at present on loan to the Canadian Railway Company who were constructing a light railway towards the front line.

* The legend was that when she fell the war would end.

The camp is a God-forsaken place; the tents are spread over the rising ground but are wet, muddy and exposed to the howling winds. We are able to get warmed up while working but at night we are almost frozen to death.

Monday, 19th March
We marched out of the Somme area and after a tiresome tramp we settled down for the night at Warloy. We had visions of a restful spell in the back areas, but it was by no means restful. We were on our way to another area.

Tuesday 20th: Marched from Warloy to Puchevillers.
Wednesday 21st: Puchevillers to Barly.
Thursday, 22nd: Barly to Ligny-sur-Canche.
Friday, 23rd: A day of rest; precious little to look at but thankful to be resting.
Saturday, 24th: Ligny-sur-Canche to Valhuon.
Sunday, 25th: Valhuon to Auchy-au-Bois.

Monday, 26th March†
Auchy-au-Bois to Vendin, about a couple of kilometres from Béthune. Our barns here are quite comfortable and our training is mostly open warfare style which requires a lot of skirmishing at night as well as by day. It is strenuous but something different. Maybe we are preparing for a breakthrough somewhere; this will be totally different from the usual trench-hopping.

Although we have marched seven days out of eight we are all feeling brighter and certainly more cheerful. We are almost human once more; it's really wonderful what a few days out of the battle area does for your spirits even though we know this respite will be brief. We have not marched all this way just for a change of air, there is something big brewing and we will be involved for certain.

Easter Sunday, 8th April
We left Vendin in a snowstorm, almost at a minute's notice and

† Three days later I was promoted to Leading Seaman.

marched to Houchin Camp. It's the usual routine, light training and plenty of local skirmishing. The weather is atrocious; the snow turned to sleet for an hour or so and then huge snow-flakes made the ice-covered roads treacherous but still we played our little game of make believe. This farce continued for the following two days but I suppose it keeps us on our toes. Anyway it is not so dangerous as the real thing and it does keep us out of trouble of a different sort.

Wednesday, 11th April
For the last four or five days there has been considerable activity on the Vimy Ridge area close by but although we are in support of the Canadians who are involved, we were not called upon. Today we were out skirmishing as usual. At 9.30 a.m., we were hurriedly recalled. In less than half-an-hour, we were on the march eventually arriving in the village of Gaucourt, roughly mid-way between Béthune and Arras. It was a long and tiresome trek but the weather was much kinder. On the following day there were no parades other than the local ones, company fatigues in and around the village. Quite a pleasant day.

Friday, 13th April
I'm not at all superstitious, having got over that nonsense long ago. Off we went again by local road to Camblain and thence by main road to Mont-St-Eloi. There was a lot of troop movement round about; some were obviously new arrivals judging by their manner and neatness. We old campaigners are not quite so spruce looking, but nevertheless full of the joy of spring with the men, rifles slung over their shoulders, arms swinging in unison and in full voice. We would show them how to march; we ought to, we have had plenty of practice lately.

Leaving the Arras road we took the local road to our right and settled down for the night in the village of Ecoivres. It is much the same as the other villages, homely but nothing to get ecstatic about.

Saturday, 14th April
Immediately after breakfast we left the village in 'Battle-order' to take up our position in the reserve trenches on the Gavrelle front,

The taking of Vimy Ridge.

more or less due west of Arras. The men we relieved were of the 34th Division, I believe. As usual when taking over a different trench system, nothing is ever quite right. What was thought suitable by the former occupants were certainly not in any way suitable for us chaps. It's a sort of disease that affects all battalion officers apparently. This must be altered at once; that too, must be changed; every damned thing must be altered. One would think that we were going to garrison this glorified ditch for the rest of the war instead of, at the most, seven or eight days. However, apart from the shelling, a spell in the reserve trenches is accepted as a cushy job.

Monday, 16th April
We relieved the 'Drake' battalion in the firing line and began the alterations all over again. At the moment this is a quiet sector. The enemy trenches are somewhere in the open belt of country between us and the village of Gavrelle and our position is at right angles to the tree-lined Arras-Gavrelle-Oppy road. Two days later, 18th April, we were relieved by 'D' company and returned to the reserve trench about two hundred yards to the rear. From here we were employed as a working party to go forward during the hours of darkness into 'No man's land' to dig a jumping-off trench well ahead of our firing line. As a Lewis-gun NCO I took my gun team in advance of the working party and occupied a shell-hole well ahead of the white tape the Engineers had laid to mark the position of the advanced trench. After satisfying myself that the spot I had selected was the best possible, I made my way over to the left to find the position of the 'B' company's gun and also the position of the 'A' company's gun at the same time advising them of my position. Satisfied that everything was in order and that each gun-team knew the whereabouts of the others, I followed the ditch alongside the roadway back to our own firing line and to report to my company commander, Lieutenant Morrison.

He appeared to be well satisfied with my report but was concerned about my return journey and asked if I would be able to locate my own gun. I said that on my way across the frontage I had stuck a rifle upwards every fifty paces. All I had to do was to locate

The opening day of the Arras offensive, 9th April 1917. Troops move out of the support trenches to take over part of the newly won position.

Canadian soldiers take their ease in the ruins of Arras.

the last rifle which I had stuck in the ditch quite close to 'A' Company's position and from then all I had to do was to count the fifty paces, lowering the rifles as I passed them. My plan worked reasonably well. At the beginning I was not always correct in my direction but near enough, I had a tendency to bear to my left but realised this was making me go closer to the enemy line than was my intention or desire. The next marker was a problem, I had overdone my correction and gone too far to my right but I found the marker eventually. Roaming about in 'No man's land' all alone in the dark was most unpleasant, I felt that the eyes of the world were upon me, half of them notably hostile and the other half at least, very suspicious. I need not to have worried but that is easier said than done.

The night was very cold with intermittent squalls of snow and sleet but otherwise quite normal. The working party returned to their reserve trench about 2 a.m. as they had been instructed and we Lewis-gun teams withdrew to the partly-dug trench and occupied it until almost dawn, about 5 a.m., in case the enemy took a fancy to it. The movement back to the firing line was done in short rushes helped along by a few shrapnel bursts. Queer stuff this shrapnel. If you are in the open, it makes you run like hell; if you happen to have the doubtful shelter of a trench, shallow or deep, you are too damned scared to move at all. This was the routine for the next three days.

CHAPTER THIRTEEN

A Comrade in Arms

Sunday, 22nd April

We were relieved by the 'Drake' battalion and moved further back to a railway cutting arriving there at two-thirty in the morning. Our stay here, in comparative safety, was extremely short. At 11 p.m. we were on our way back to the newly dug assembly trenches in readiness for the coming attack. Zero hour was to be 4.45 a.m., and obviously the attacking troops had to be in position much earlier to allow the support troops and the reserves to be positioned also. At 1.30 we were occupying our section in the jumping-off trench some considerable distance in front of our firing line.

I took up a position in a small shell-crater about ten yards or so ahead of the assembled troops. The terrain was quite flat and open unlike the moonscape of the Somme and Ancre, and absolutely ideal for Tank operation if we had had any, but we didn't. It was also ideal for machine-gun fire, reaping an easy harvest of the advancing infantrymen and we knew the enemy had plenty of machine-guns.

The night started very cold but it became a little warmer as we lay in the open with nothing to do for the next three hours or so apart from trying to kid ourselves that we had not been observed. Occasional shells that passed over were taken for granted to be the beginning of a defensive bombardment against which we had no shelter, nor had the thousands of men lying in the open close behind us. If the enemy had had any inkling of what was in store for them, then every shell-burst would have reaped a rich harvest.

I reported my position to my company commander, Lieutenant Morrison. He was always meticulous about the whereabouts of his Lewis guns. He was a grand officer and a good listener at all times to suggestions or complaints. As I was about to go forward to my gun-team, he told me that our Colonel, B.C. Freyberg VC, had been appointed Brigadier of the London Division and was taking up his appointment at once. Commander A.M. Asquith DSO who had recovered from his wounds on the Ancre and had been appointed to the Intelligence Staff of the Third Army but had requested several times permission to rejoin his old battalion, was to lead the 'Hood' in the attack.

As an 'old hand', I had been over the top on many occasions on Gallipoli and on the Western Front under the leadership of both Colonel Freyberg and Lieutenant Commander Asquith. The last minute change of leadership on the eve of the attack would in no way affect the result. We were extremely sorry to lose our famous Colonel but no promotion could have been more richly deserved. We knew Commander Asquith and would follow him to Hell if he so wished. My personal opinion for what is is worth, is that had Commander Asquith not been the Prime Minister's son, he too would have been awarded the Army's highest honour; he certainly earned it.

The order of the attack was that the 'Hood' battalion should not move forward until the barrage lifted off the enemy's front line trenches. Commander Asquith knew from past experience, perfectly well, as we old campaigners also knew, that roughly five or six minutes after the opening of our bombardment, the enemy would open up on 'No man's land' to prevent our supporting troops coming forward to reinforce us.

The directing of a battle from a position miles behind may have been convenient on Salisbury Plain during peacetime manoeuvres but in modern warfare, with the massive concentration of artillery and machine-gun fire, remote control is hopelessly out of date as are the brass-hats who issue these suicidal orders.

At the opening of the Battle of the Somme on 1st July after seven days and nights of continuous bombardment, it was thought by the High Command that the enemy resistance would be nil. The attacking men would simply walk over and occupy the undefended enemy lines. They issued an order that the attacking troops would walk at a steady pace of not more than fifty yards a minute. If there happened to be any resistance, they were not to run until they were within twenty yards of the enemy line so that they would not get exhausted! The first wave moved forward at seven-thirty in brilliant sunshine three hours after dawn so that the artillery observers could have a clear view of what was happening. Throughout the whole of my training and experience it was drilled into me that speed was always the controlling factor, yet these poor chaps were ordered to go forward at a snail's pace by the High Command, well, the observers got their clear view and there was plenty to see. The pride of Kitchener's volunteer army and many Regular Army Divisions were annihilated within the first hour. Over twenty-one thousand lay dead and over thirty-five thousand were wounded. Wave after wave of young men from every town and village in the country were ordered forward and were cut down like ripe corn at harvest-time on this very ground in former, peacetime days. Very few, and in many cases none at all, reached the enemy trenches. Those that did were entangled in the mass of barbed-wire, uncut by the million-and-a-half shells fired by nearly one-thousand-and-a-half guns during the seven day bombardment. The thirty-feet deep dugouts withstood the bombardment because of the shortage of heavy calibre shells. The shrapnel, if the timing of the fuse was a fraction too early, burst harmlessly above the wire, if the timing was a fraction too late, the shells buried themselves deep in the ground leaving the wire untouched or making it even more entangled if that were possible.

That was the price we paid for remote control. Any divisional officer or battalion officer was capable of much better strategy. They were on the spot with their men and so many of them are still there, enriching the soil of France, not eight miles away in a comfortable château playing with little red flags. Those of us of the 'Hood' battalion who survived the battle for Gavrelle, owe our lives to our commander who ignored the order to wait until the barrage lifted from the enemy front line and ordered us to attack immediately the barrage opened, and what is more he was among the first troops to enter the village. In roughly ten minutes we had captured our first objective, the enemy trench immediately in front of the village. I had a feeling that a lot of our casualties were sustained through our being too close to our own barrage as quite a lot of the shells were falling short but, had we not ignored the order to wait, our losses would have been ruinous. The curtain of fire behind us was even worse than the inferno in the village ahead.

It took us fifteen minutes to sort ourselves out as arranged, before we went forward to our second objective, a road running approximately north and south through the village. We kept close to the creeping wall of fire but it was impossible to keep in touch with each other as we scrambled over, and sometimes under the ruins, blinded by the brick dust, bombarded by flying timbers, machined-gunned and sniped from cellars, scattered by shell-bursts. We eventually reached our objective, though in small groups.

In my bunch there were men of the 'Nelson' battalion, 'Bedfords' and 'Hoods' all mixed up. The plan was for the artillery to blast hell out of that part of the village still held by the enemy while we reorganised. I don't know who formulates these plans but, whoever they are, they seem to think the enemy will cease fighting and 'stand-at-ease' whilst their attackers reorganise for another bash at them. What really happens is that the enemy knows exactly where we are, concentrates his troops, reserves and artillery fire where he knows they will do the most damage, making reorganising virtually impossible. They still have the shelter of their trenches whilst we are in the open; their artillery has a shorter range; point-blank in some places, whilst our field-guns are now out of effective range to be of much use to us. The moment we leave the shelter of the pile of bricks, a German in a cellar a few feet away, probably more scared than me, doesn't wait for me to prod him with my bayonet; he just presses the trigger with no need to take aim. The one that is quickest on the draw is the one that survives.

We hopped about among the ruins for what seemed ages trying to form some sort of a line, but had no success at all because of the shelling, sniping and machine-gun fire. It was finally decided that when our barrage lifted according to plan we would follow it the best we could. It would be every man for himself. The age of the officer, his head partially covered with a blood-stained bandage, waving his sword and urging his men forward, so beautifully portrayed in the *Illustrated London News* during the Boer War, went out on 4th August 1914. The machine-gun, which Lord Kitchener insisted was a new-fangled toy, respected neither officer or man and the casualty lists made this point quite clear. A sub-lieutenant was lying among the ruins where I and my bunch were sheltering. He was there when we arrived; his uniform was in shreds and a piece of barbed wire was entangled round what was left of one of his legs, his face bespattered with grime and brick dust deep red in colour, partially obscured a sinister grin. He was not alone, only one of the thousands Rupert Brooke had in mind before he himself died on active service while serving in my battalion exactly two years ago this very day:

Poured out the red
Sweet wine of youth; gave up the years to be
Of work and joy, and that unhoped serene
That men call age.

Our third and final objective was just beyond the village. The barrage was moving slowly forward, groups of dust-covered men were endeavouring to find the easiest way through the smoke-covered ruins. The bursting of the shells, mostly heavy stuff, severely hampered our progress. At times we were unable to see each other through the clouds of smoke and brick-dust, the fumes from the detonations were making us all cough and spit as we overran the huge piles of rubble that were once the proud homes and possessions of the peaceful villagers. In such a scene one cannot avoid feeling nostalgic; such a lovely sunny morning to be surrounded by so much death and wanton destruction. Oh, for home and beauty, *Deo Volente*.

Our progress was very slow. With our eyes everywhere, our minds blank to everything except self-preservation, we staggered forward crab-like, individually yet all the time trying to keep within sight of our pals. I felt more composed when someone was near me. I suppose we all have that feeling, but time and time again I found myself alone and wondering where everyone had got to. Immediately in front of me there appeared to be a group of our chaps making their way parallel with the main street towards a large building which I believe was the Mayor's house. The time was getting on for seven o'clock when I joined them; they were apparently awaiting orders but I could not see any officers; in fact, I could not see anyone on my right flank at all.

After a few minutes we all moved forward up towards the Mayor's house. My rifle was slung over my left shoulder, my left hand was in my trouser pocket to prevent my rifle slipping off. As a leading seaman in charge of Lewis Guns, I had been issued with a revolver but I always had my rifle with me as well when in action.

I had moved forward only a few yards when I noticed a rifle barrel moving among a pile of ruins only a yard or so away. I turned instinctively to my left and fired my revolver as I did so. I didn't need the smoke from the barrel of the rifle to tell me I had been hit. The impact forced me to turn round several times, the pain in my left wrist was excruciating. I have often heard it said that men sometimes don't realise that they have been wounded. Maybe this is true if it is just a flesh wound but when a red-hot bullet at point blank range goes through the bone taking the splinters with it and makes the exit hole ten times larger than the entry, it's a different matter. The whole of my arm was paralysed, I was unable to withdraw my hand from my pocket.

After a few moments I realised that I was extremely vulnerable so I moved a few steps forward and found my adversary at the entrance of a half filled cellar. He was still clutching his rifle but half his head was blown away. I had long since got over the embarrassment of having a corpse for a companion for it happens all the time. The continuous banging and crashing of the shells with the resultant showers of flying debris obliterates any sentimental thoughts. I had but one desire, one aim; to survive. I had reached the point that I was beginning to think it was most unlikely. To put it bluntly I was scared stiff.

How long I remained cornered like a rat I do not know, other than it was some considerable time during which I cogitated on what my next move would be as soon as the shelling eased up a bit; if I lived that long. After many anxious moments I decided to get to hell out of there. I set off hoping to make the road that ran through the village as my first dash but, as Robbie Burns wrote in his 'To a mouse': 'The best laid schemes o' mice and men, Gang aft a-gley'. Dodging in and around the piles of rubble and taking the utmost advantage of the shelter they provided, I failed to locate the road but came across an almost untouched cellar fairly deep and quite roomy as well. After a cursory glance I satisfied myself that I was the master of the house, at least that part of it that was left. I would be quite safe here for a while, I thought, and settled down for a much needed rest. Unfortunately, as the saying goes, there's no rest for the wicked, almost immediately a very loud detonation blew me head over heels. I thought at first that it was a shell burst but as I hurriedly scrambled out I observed that a wave of troops had passed over on their way to reinforce the men who by now had captured their final objective just beyond the village. The detonation had most likely came from a Mills bomb thrown by one of the advancing men who was not taking any chances of being shot in the back as they moved forward. I've done the same thing many times myself; after all, he was not to know that the only occupant of the cellar was 'a wee, sleeket, cowrin', tim'rous beastie'.

I began to wonder what would happen if another wave of our chaps coming forward, their vision blurred by the clouds of smoke and brick-dust, what their reactions would be if they saw a very frightened and begrimed young fellow, not yet come of age, prowling about the ruins on his own. Time and time again there are occasions when one is in more danger from one's own men than from the enemy. I was fully aware that I might not be the only prowler and we might not be on the same side. The sooner I get away from these ruins the more hopeful I would feel of survival.

While in the cellar before I was so rudely disturbed, I had attempted to get some life back into my left arm but only succeeded in increasing the flow of warm blood down my leg. As the shelling appeared to be less severe now I reluctantly left my haven and made some progress in short rushes through the ruins. Other than getting as far away from the inferno as I could, my direction was dictated by what appeared to me to be the best shelter if the shelling increased. Eventually I was clear of the ruins and realised that I had unknowingly crossed the road that I was looking for, and that I was now in the original enemy front line, battered almost beyond recognition. It had been the target for our artillery at the opening of the barrage and no doubt much of the damage had resulted from the direct hits of our heavies and by now, since the enemy had lost possession, they, in turn, had done their best to prevent us enjoying the fruits of their labours. The result was a very irregular line of shell-craters joined by short strips of trench and not a healthy place to linger. My escape route from here was over more than half-a-mile of open ground, flat and in full view of the enemy still holding the high ground as usual, beyond the village.

I tried to figure out the pattern of their shelling and decided to move a little closer to the main road to Arras before venturing to cross the open ground. I made several hurried hops from one shell-hole to another when to my utter amazement, I landed in one occupied by a young German about my age. He made no attempt to move, maybe because I was pointing my revolver at him. Normally I would have pressed the trigger without the slightest compunction even if I had not been winged. Why I hesitated I do not know. At that moment I had no love for mine enemy; the only good German was a dead one. Live and let live was out of date, kill or be killed was the order of the day. Yet all my anger had deserted me and the pain in my wrist had gone with it.

I tried to converse with him but to no avail; there was no response at all. He looked so helpless, so pitiful and his vague look, not a stare; haunted me to distraction. The incessant singing of the bullets overhead, the annoying regularity of the shell-bursts quite near with the resultant shower of hot metal and earth clods falling like hail around us made no impression on that frozen enigmatical countenance.

A dull, ominous thud close-by made the ground quiver so much that my rifle slid away from my shoulder coming to rest across my prisoner's stomach. I beckoned with my revolver for him to move it away very gently and slowly. To attempt to do this myself would have meant my losing the effectiveness of my revolver and leave me vulnerable if he attempted to take advantage of the situation. In spite of my gestures it was some moments before he plucked up sufficient courage to move his hands towards me but with further encouragement, he very slowly and gently eased the offending rifle away from him and at the same time drew my attention to my blood-stained touser leg as if to tell me something I had known for quite sometime. He made signs that he had something that might be of help to me in his pocket.

A curt nod from me brought a distinct ray of hope to his icy eyes; he was no longer afraid of what I might do to him and was anxious to help me. He cautiously produced a fairly large piece of rag from somewhere about his person and, by his subsequent actions, obviously thought that it was my thigh that needed attention. I perceived a slight smile behind that iron mask when I pointed to my wrist.

He instantly tore the seam of my trouser leg to the waist which liberated my hand with the pocket quite firmly attached by the congealed blood. It also allowed the release of my rifle sling. To my great relief I was able to move my arm again but had no feeling whatsoever in my hand.

During all this first-aid treatment I had replaced my revolver in its holster. The lad could have butted me with his head if he had so desired but he was more concerned with my wound, now bleeding much too freely for my liking. He extracted the pad of gauze from my emergency dressing and carefully placed it over the exit hole – cavity would be a better description – in my wrist. Then, with the dexterity of a professional nurse who would have received the approval of Florence Nightingale, he completed the bandaging in a few moments. The rag was not long enough to serve as a proper sling but after a moment's hesitation, he threaded one end of it through the top buttonhole of my tunic and knotted it with the other end thus forming a loop that served as a sling. With my hand raised in this position I felt much more comfortable and certainly more mobile but extremely weak.

By this time the enemy were concentrating their artillery fire on the village just a little behind us and I decided it was a time to get further away to the rear towards our assembly trenches. Bearing in mind that a soldier's best friend was his rifle I gathered mine from the mud knowing full well that I could not effectively use the damned thing with only one hand. Nevertheless I felt safer with it.

With a casual nod to my prisoner, and with his dumb approval I am sure, we set off in short rushes from one shell-hole to another, always keeping close to each other. I think that he felt safer with me and I felt safer after each frantic dash. Several times we were sprayed with earth from the nearby shell bursts but our luck so far gave me courage to get the most out of every dash. The further away from the raging battle the more daring we became Of course, we were a long way from being out of danger as the enemy were blanketing the whole area with shrapnel and some heavy stuff as we reached our assembly trenches at this point barely two feet deep and hardly recognizable. The shallowness of these trenches where the whole of the attacking force had spent most of the night made me realise how fortunate we all were that our presence there was unknown to the enemy as the amount of shelter was really negligible.

I would have liked to rest awhile as I was feeling very exhausted, but decided to push on to our original firing line as there would be much more shelter there, for it was much deeper. At least, that's what I thought but, on reaching it after many enforced crouchings in shell-holes, I found to my dismay that it had been blasted out of all recognition since I had left it many hours previously. However, at the moment the enemy was most obliging; his shelling was desultory and centred mainly on the Arras road some distance to our right. I had planned originally to make for the deep ditch that ran along it that I knew to be there having taken advantage of it the night before we attacked but the shelling made me change my plans.

I stumbled over the open ground hoping to come across the railway cutting I had spent a little time the day before the attack. The going was very hard. I was so weary and fell over several times and had to be assisted up by my prisoner. We eventually reached the cutting arm in arm. The war seemed miles away because of the shelter the deep cutting afforded us and I was so drowsy, I had used up all my energy and unconsciously closed my eyes feeling safe at last and very pleased with myself having once more survived another terrible ordeal. I doubt if I actually slept more than a few seconds; it was such a relief, but my thoughts were again fixed on my comrades still fighting for their lives, those friends whose fighting days are over and the ordeal of the people back home.

During my short leave seven months ago, I had seen the effect of the war of attrition on the people of my mining village; almost every family had lost someone very dear to them; some more than one; many I had gone to school with. Some of my pals that had survived the terrible ordeal of the Gallipoli campaign, the slaughter on the Somme and the Ancre were still involved in the holocaust within hearing distance, there seemed to be no end. Even during my few days' leave, three of those dreaded telegrams arrived; one was actually delivered whilst I was calling upon a boy's father who, before the war, had been crippled for life in an accident at the local mine where we, all three of us, had worked. I had the feeling that my presence at that moment made matters even worse. I have never felt so helpless in all my life.

Those were my thoughts as I trudged along the railway cutting away from the battle, though still not out of danger by any means. I had on my own accord volunteered for service; I anticipated the going would be rough as the old veterans of the Boer War had constantly told us youngsters of their experiences. I did not expect to be molly-coddled. I accepted my fate but, for those poor souls back home, the uncertainty that overshadowed every moment of their lives, must have been crucifying. As a fighting man I don't think I was alone in my thoughts. We were all very tight-lipped about such matters but, however secretive, we always knew what was uppermost in our minds. In the heat of battle we are concerned only with survival, we become wild animals, we cease to be human beings, we go forth blindly, the margin between bravery and madness is very narrow. In war we repeatedly commit acts that in peace-time would be rewarded with the hangman's rope, but such acts in time of war are considered heroic. My brain has become so contorted that, try as I may, there are times that I cannot differentiate between what is right and what is wrong. One moment I am filled with blood-thirsty anger and the next I'm filled with remorse playing havoc with my soul.

At the present I am really insane with joy. I'm alive and the man with me is also alive in spite of my intention to blast him to eternity the moment I clapped eyes on him. Yet during the last few hectic hours we have been helping each other in every possible way. For my part I am truly grateful for the way he has helped me.

Whilst we are still very much in the danger area and so long as he is with me as a prisoner-of-war, his fighting days are over. Instead of being his executioner, I am his guardian angel but, without me, in all probability he would have been shot on sight as an enemy sniper. As for myself, I am afraid that my still bleeding wound would cost me my place in the first team maybe for quite a considerable time.

The pace of my thoughts has far exceeded the tempo of my aching legs. As we approached the Arras-Gavrelle road, however, I came across a spacious shelter cut in the embankment. By its position it was obviously constructed by the enemy and originally occupied by them in former days. Within a few seconds of our arrival at this haven of rest, I was offered a mug of sergeant-major's really strong, piping hot tea which I shared with my now slightly apprehensive prisoner. The short rest and the most refreshing drink I had ever tasted in my life, gave me boundless energy; I was on top of the world and raring to go on my way to the nearest dressing station which I was told was at St Catherine on the fringe of Arras.

'Just bear to your right as you enter Arras, Good luck, matey.'

It was quite a long stretch but all the shelling and the falling debris was behind us. We were frequently offered mugs of tea and enjoyed every sip plus the many friendly pats on the back. We had almost reached Arras when a spotless sergeant came between me and my prisoner, and in a most officious manner told me he would see 'this bastard off from now on'. At the same time he roughly pushed to one side the man who had helped me to get so far.

'You carry on. I will see this bastard off,' he repeated.

At this precise moment I thought I should make sure that my loaded revolver was still in working order and, in doing so, forgot the standing rule, never, never point a fire-arm towards anyone, especially officious sergeants, during inspection. Careless of me, I know, but I have never in my life seen a sergeant skedaddle so quickly out of sight. Without further interference we arrived at the dressing station and were met by the most humane sergeant in the

(*Left*) Myself, as a leading seaman, with companions at the Marquis of Bath's country home, Longleat, after being wounded for the second time at the battle of Gavrelle on 23rd April 1917. (*Right*) Back in the Navy 1917.

Staff and patients at Beaufort War Hospital, Bristol in 1917.

whole army. He listened to my account of the last few hours and gave me his solemn promise that my enemy comrade-in-arms would receive his personal attention. I surrendered my fire-arms and equipment as ordered.

Prisoner and winged escort had a mug of tea together then with a warm handshake, we went on our separate ways, never to meet again in person, but I often think of him.

After my wound had been cleaned and dressed I was inoculated and then conveyed by bus to the 3rd Casualty Clearing Station and thence by train to the 22nd General, at Camiers, arriving a little after midnight and feeling very pleased with myself.

Tuesday; 24th April

After a good night's rest and a hearty breakfast, and after my wound had been dressed and cleaned up, I lined up with the others for inspection by the Chief Medical Officer. After a very thorough but gentle examination, I left with my forearm in a sling and comfortably splinted. A label had been pinned on my tunic marked 'Hospital Ship Deck'. As a 'walking wounded' I was able to move about freely and, in doing so, came across many of the Royal Naval Division in similar circumstances as myself but most of them had been more severely knocked about than I had been. Without exception though, we were all happy to be receiving such expert medical care.

Wednesday, 25th April

Exactly two years ago I was a member of the 'suicide party' who accompanied Lieutenant B.C. Freyberg when he alone swam ashore and ignited flares in the Bulair Lines area of the Gallipoli Peninsula, for which he was awarded the first of his DSOs. He subsequently was awarded the Victoria Cross during our attack on Beaumont Hamel-Beaucourt-sur-Ancre on 13th November 1916.

Later today I again lined up for inspection by the Commanding Officer. While we were waiting in the long queue, word was passed down the line for those wearing splints not to remove them or interfere with them in any way; all other cases were to remove their bandages ready for inspection. As I was wearing a splint I did as I was told but on nearing the officer, the Matron, a real battle-axe type if ever there was one, brusquely ordered me to remove my bandages, for what reason I will never know. However after inspection, the splint was replaced and my label endorsed 'H.S. Deck' remained.

Friday, 27th April
At three o'clock in the morning with more tickets pinned to my tunic, we were conveyed by bus to the station and thence by train to Calais to board the hospital ship *Cambria*. After a wait of about two hours, during which many more wounded came aboard, we sailed in brilliant sunshine and a calm sea, arriving in Dover harbour at four in the evening. It was round about eight p.m. when my turn came to leave the ship and board a waiting train that was to take us to Bristol.

Saturday, 28th April
At five o'clock in the morning we were welcomed by Sister Williams in Beaufort War Hospital and immediately given a postcard to write to my parents to let them know of my arrival in England.

'They will be pleased with your news,' said Sister Williams.

How extremely thoughtful of her!